Allen Warren, with the inquisitiveness of a historian, opens many windows into the life of Eric Milner-White to provide the first thorough assessment of his gifts and complexities. We encounter far more than the Milner-White of Nine Lessons and Carols as we see into this twentieth-century Dean's quest for the beauty of holiness through art, music, architecture, stained glass and, above all, the crafting of prayers.

Graham Usher
Bishop of Norwich

—

This book is not just a study of the churchman who made a college service into the intangible patrimony of the entire English-speaking world. It is the portrait of an era. When the Church of England was led by some of the cleverest and the bravest in our country. When the hyper-privileged organized missions to the poorest in our society. When the established Church was a key part of the Establish-ment. When the bases of our modern university system were being laid, and heritage conservation became a political imperative. When major public figures had very private lives. And when an unmarried Dean, with a taste for the ballet, charming young men and ceramics, could pass without comment.

Neil MacGregor
art historian

More than Nine Lessons and Carols

A Life of Eric Milner-White, 1884–1963

— ALLEN WARREN —

Sacristy
Press

Sacristy Press
PO Box 612, Durham, DH1 9HT

www.sacristy.co.uk

First published in 2025 by Sacristy Press, Durham

Sacristy Limited, registered in England & Wales, number 7565667

British Library Cataloguing-in-Publication Data
A catalogue record for the book is available from the British Library

ISBN 978-1-78959-397-6

Contents

Illustrations

Section 1

1. Harrow school boy. Private collection.
2. Oscar Browning, Milner's tutor. Vanity Fair, 24 November 1888; © National Portrait Gallery. Used with permission.
3. Ernest Arthur Edghill (1879–1912), Milner's most important Southwark friend. Daily Mirror, 23 August 1912.
4. Milner as a young priest, c.1910; © The Provost and Fellows of King's College, Cambridge. Used with permission.
5. Milner as army chaplain, no date; © The Provost and Fellows of King's College, Cambridge. Used with permission.
6. Anglo-Catholic Congress, 1920. Opening procession along Holborn, 29 June 1920. From the Souvenir of the First Anglo-Catholic Congress (1920), digitally republished by Project Canterbury, 2015, by Richard Mammana from a copy belonging to the Rt Rev Dr Terry M. Brown.
7. Milner as "Arch" in the Choristers' Camp, mid 1930s. Used with permission of The Friends of York Minster.
8. Milner as Dean of York 1941–63. Used with permission of the Dean and Chapter, York Minster.
9. Hans Hess (1907–75), Curator, York City Art Gallery, c.1965. Photo: Virgil Lucky.
10. Philip Loyd (1884–1952), Trappist, lifelong friend, and bishop, R.P. Stacy Waddy, Philip Loyd: Missionary and Bishop (Oxford: Mowbray's, 1954), frontispiece.
11. Arthur Michael Ramsey, Archbishop of York 1956–61 and Archbishop of Canterbury 1961–74.
12. Milner as York Minster restorer. Used with permission of the Dean and Chapter, York Minster.

13. Milner, the collector of pots. © National Portrait Gallery. Used with permission.
14. The Leaping Salmon 1931 by Bernard Leach (1887–1979), City of York Art Gallery. Used with permission.
15. Milner as elderly Dean of York. Used with permission of the Dean and Chapter, York Minster.

Section 2

16. Bitterne: (a) New church at Bitterne © Sotonepedia; (b) Bitterne, Window in the new church. Photo by the author.
17. Rouen Window, sixteenth century, acquired by St Mary's Church, Rickmansworth from St Jean, Rouen. Later removed and in store in 1952. Purchased by Milner-White and installed in York Minster [window s6] as a memorial to his friend Philip Loyd and his brother, Lewis.
18. Harry Stammers in his workshop. © Henry Hinchcliffe. Used with permission.
19. Window in St Nicholas, Withernsea, East Yorkshire (1947). © Henry Hinchcliffe. Used with permission. Stammers comments, "The feelings in play here; Jesus' compassion, the woman's contrition . . . are almost palpable.".
20. Window in St Nicholas, Hollym, East Yorkshire (1948). © Henry Hinchcliffe. Used with permission. An unusual example of Stammers making full use of clear glass, allowing the visual context of the church to be internally and externally illuminated.
21. St Andrew, Bishopthorpe, York (1950). © Henry Hinchcliffe. "The Church as provider of education throughout the ages" (Harry Stammers).
22. St Matthias Church, Stocksbridge, South Yorkshire (1950). © Henry Hinchcliffe. "My brothers the birds, much ought ye to praise your Creator" (Francis of Assisi).
23. St Martin's Church, Firbeck, Nottinghamshire (1953). © Henry Hinchcliffe. Six parables in glass.

24. St Helen's Church, Welton, East Yorkshire (1954). © Henry Hinchcliffe. "A celebration of Church music" (Harry Stammers).
25. Christ Church, Wadsley Bridge, Sheffield (1957). © Henry Hinchcliffe. "A Litany of Labour in glass", the panel directly reflecting agriculture and industry in contemporary dress, rather than the complete window.
26. St Michael's College, Llandaff (1959). © Henry Hinchcliffe. A unique example of Stammers' work in a new church and in collaboration with George Pace.
27. York College for Girls, York, North Yorkshire (1960). "The third shepherd, with the red cloak, is a portrait of Eric Milner-White, Dean of York. This window is now in the Merchant Adventurers' Hall, York." (Harry Stammers).
28. North Riding Mental Hospital, York (1949). © Henry Hinchcliffe. A moving institutional tableau in glass, now poorly re-instated in the Chapel of York District Hospital.

Preface, and Notes on Sources and Acknowledgements

This study of Eric Milner-White has had a lengthy history, initiated by a York-based charity, the Sheldon Memorial Trust, of which the author has been a member, chairing its lectures subcommittee until recently. Oliver Sheldon was a prominent York citizen from the 1930s until his premature death in 1951. Among his many civic achievements were the founding of the York Georgian Society in 1938 and the York Civic Trust in 1946. The latter spearheaded the campaign over a 15-year period to secure a university for the city, eventually successful in 1960, and opening in 1963.

The author was in the second wave of appointments within the Department of History in 1971 and remained at the university for the next 40 years, including seven years as head of the History Department.

This latter role drew him into the civic history of the city and led to him being invited to join the Sheldon Memorial Trust, which is committed to extending the understanding of York's civic traditions and history among its citizens. The Trust agreed to reinvigorate its annual lecture, initially with a series on those individuals who had made a significant impact on the city in the 25 years following the Second World War. Unsurprisingly, many such individual lives had been lost within the collective civic memory by 2010. After much to-ing and fro-ing, I agreed to give the lecture on Eric Milner-White (Dean of York from 1941 until his death in 1963) in the autumn of 2019, a few months before the Covid pandemic.

The Trust wishes to publish each of its annual lectures and usually it has done so in collaboration with the Borthwick Institute for Archives, now part of the University of York. The author extends his deep gratitude to both directors in this period, and all their professional staff. They have been unfailingly helpful and indulgent.

A necessary preliminary to being able to give and publish the lecture was to see if there were scholars interested in particular aspects of Milner's long and varied priestly life. As a result, the Sheldon Memorial Trust hosted a one-day seminar on Milner-White at the University of York in 2016, sending out a preliminary call for papers from the late Bishop Geoffrey Rowell and myself. This prompted a wider interest than we had expected and resulted in a day of uniformly informative contributions, which were recorded. Most of these have not been subsequently published, but the author is absolutely indebted to them for the elements in Milner's life well outside his area of scholarly expertise.[1] This was particularly the case in the sections on his distinctive composition of prayers, personal, liturgical, and national. In addition, the specific treatment of York Minster's glass, his unique collection of pots, as well as paintings, church furnishings, and other art works, and his relationship with the city and its civic elites have all been enhanced by the specialist knowledge of others. A list of those contributors is provided below (see Appendix 1).

The author wishes to acknowledge fully his debt to his collaborators on that day, including the then Archbishop of York, John Sentamu, who introduced the day. Sarah Sheils, present chair of the Sheldon Memorial Trust's lectures subcommittee, has been continuously supportive, especially in her knowledge of the city's art gallery.

All studies of individual lives and careers have their specific challenges as well as those generic to the genre. This was particularly true in the case of Eric Milner-White; a moderately prominent Anglo-Catholic priest from 1918, the Dean of King's College, Cambridge until 1941, and then Dean of York until his death in 1963. He was also significant nationally during the 1920s in association with the Anglo-Catholic Congresses held between 1920 and 1933. He was a prolific writer of prayers and an innovative liturgist, including most famously the annual "Special Service" of Nine Lessons and Carols that he prepared six weeks after the Armistice in 1918. Less well known was his role in some of the more prominent

---

[1]   A recording was made of the contributions to the seminar and is available through the Sheldon Memorial Trust (see website). As usual in these cases, those wishing to use material contained will need to sign the relevant copyright documents.

National Days of Prayer held throughout the Second World War, most notably in May 1940, and at the time of D-Day in 1944.

Throughout his life, he had a very distinctive personality, at Harrow as head of his house for three years, as an undergraduate at King's from 1903 until 1907, and as a chaplain on the Western Front, naming his horse Chrysoprasus, as well as winning the DSO, technically as a non-combatant. As a characterful Dean of King's for 23 years, he was much caricatured in the college undergraduate magazine *Basileon*, as well as supporting the many considering ordination.[2]

On his rather unexpected move to York as dean in 1941, he quickly made his mark in the city, even though he possessed no significant previous parochial or diocesan experience. The theatricality of his personality was well suited to cathedral worship in a historic and beautiful city, and he pioneered his own interpretation of what a civic dean might be, elements of which featured strongly in the city council's very successful Yorkshire Festival of Britain in 1951. In addition, through the York Civic Trust founded in 1946, of which he was joint secretary, he chaired the trust's academic subcommittee in campaigning for a university to be founded in the city. He also, controversially, reinstated, and restored York Minster's medieval stained glass after 1945.

An aesthete by temperament, he was active in supporting the development of the city's art gallery in the same period, through his knowledge and taste as well as by his own gifts and financial donations, especially much of his personal collection of Japanese twentieth-century pottery on his death. He became a fanatical enthusiast for classical ballet, a collector of books—especially of contemporary detective fiction—and expert on garden heathers.

But behind all these spheres of interest, personal, religious, and artistic, he remained an enigma, seen by some as scheming, devious, and imperious, but irritatingly usually getting his own way. This elusiveness has continued since his death, as he destroyed all his personal papers, firstly those relating to his experiences as an army chaplain in the First

---

2   Chrysoprasus (Revelation 21:19–20)—a precious stone. Patrick Wilkinson, *Eric Milner-White, 1884–1963, Fellow, Chaplain and Dean, Dean of York* (Cambridge: King's College, 1963), p. 11.

World War, and later almost everything else in a long life, probably shortly before his death in 1963.

Not surprisingly this varied public life, without the dimension of the private, personal, or familiar, has deterred scholars and biographers. No entry appeared in the later twentieth-century volumes of the *Dictionary of National Biography* until its reworking and republishing as the *Oxford Dictionary of National Biography* in 2004. A jointly authored memoir, written by Philip Pare and Donald Harris, both priests and earlier undergraduates at King's and Cuddesdon, with a reflective epilogue by Archbishop Michael Ramsey, was published in 1965. Some additional privately printed tributes were published immediately following his death, and in 1991 a collection of personal accounts from younger men and women, who mainly knew him in the later years of his life, was published by the Friends of York Minster. That is all there is.

Other than these personal memoirs and reflections, the only aspects of his life studied since his death are in specialist studies of his collection of twentieth-century Japanese pots and in the history of the Festival of Nine Lessons and Carols that he initiated on Christmas Eve in 1918.

These complexities have undoubtedly shaped the volume that follows.

In beginning to work on the 2019 Sheldon lecture, on which this volume is based, it became immediately apparent that among those surviving, who had known him personally, Milner-White had divided opinion during his own lifetime. For Henry Stapleton, later Dean of Carlisle, who had been secretary of the York Diocesan Advisory Committee as a young priest, he was the "ideal" dean. To others, like John West-Taylor, secretary to the academic subcommittee of the York Civic Trust, which Milner-White chaired, he was not entirely trusted, according to John's widow.[3]

This ambiguity is reflected most strikingly in the views of two archbishops of York, both of whom had known Milner-White. The first was Michael Ramsey, who had met him as a boy in the 1920s, writing an epilogue to the Pare and Harris tribute in 1965 as Archbishop of Canterbury. For Ramsey, taught divinity by Milner-White at King's College School in the 1920s, he had been an inspiration; he retained a

---

[3]   Private information.

photograph of him in his study throughout his life. The other was John Habgood, Archbishop of York (1983–95), who had known Milner-White as a young Fellow of King's in the 1950s, not yet ordained. Approached in 2012 to comment on Milner-White, he declined. Pressed privately to say why, he replied that the younger Fellows thought him rather "ridiculous" on his occasional visits as a Life Fellow, with his mannered speech, and his habit of calling King's "this blessed place".[4]

As the reader will discover, these tensions among those analysing his character and actions are threads through his whole life.

---

[4]   Private information.

Abbreviations

BNA The British Newspaper Archive (The British Library in association with Find My Past Ltd. ongoing).

KCAC King's College, Cambridge Archive Centre.

ODCC F. L. Cross and E. A. Livingstone (eds), *The Oxford Dictionary of the Christian Church*, 3rd edn (Oxford: University/Clarendon Press, 1997).

ODNB H. C. G. Matthew and Brian Harrison (eds), *The Oxford Dictionary of National Biography: In Association with the British Academy: From the Earliest Times to the Year 2000* (Oxford: Clarendon Press, 2004).

YML York Minster Library.

Sources

Manuscripts

Milner-White Papers

These are voluminous but uneven, as Milner destroyed all personal material during his lifetime, including that of his parents. What survives are his working papers in a long and active life held in the archives of York Minster and in King's College, Cambridge Archive Centre.

Similarly, most of those who knew Milner personally left no surviving correspondence of any size. The one exception is the collection of Milner's letters as an undergraduate and young priest to Oscar Browning, his undergraduate tutor at King's from 1903 until 1907, a connection that continued until 1914—about twenty letters in all.

As doubtless he intended, the historian is forced to rely on institutional and public material at every stage of Milner-White's life; home, family, and schooling, 1884–1903; King's College, Cambridge 1903–7, 1912–14; Woolwich 1908–12; France and Italy 1914–18; King's College, Cambridge as Dean 1918–41; and York Minster as Dean 1941–63.

Printed sources

With this lack of personal material, it is not surprising that his life has attracted little published interest, except for the brief period after his death among those who knew and worked with him. These are:

Wilkinson, Patrick, *Eric Milner-White, 1884–1963, Fellow, Chaplain and Dean, Dean of York* (Cambridge: King's College, Cambridge, privately printed, 1963).
Referred to in the text as Wilkinson, *Milner-White*.
Pare, Philip, and Harris, Donald, with an epilogue by Archbishop Michael Ramsey, *Milner-White: A Memoir 1884–1963* (London: SPCK, 1965).

Referred to in the text as Pare and Harris, *Milner-White: A Memoir*.

Holtby, Robert (ed.), *Eric Milner-White: A Memorial* (York: Friends of York Minster, 1991).

Referred to in the text as Holtby, *Milner-White: A Memorial*.

Nicholson, J. Malcolm, *Eric Milner-White, 1884–1963* (Tynemouth: King's School, 1963).

Nicholson, J. Malcolm, *Milner and his Benjamin: An Account of Eric Milner-White and his Dealings with King's School, Tynemouth* (Hexham: Peter Robson, pr. 1975).

McMullen, Alan John, *Eric Milner-White* (York: Dean and Chapter, York Minster, 1984), Friends of York Minster Annual Report, 1984. [YML RR BAY 6 PER:FRI].

McMullen, Alan John, *Obituary: The Very Reverend Eric Milner-White* (London: British Society of Glass-Painters, 1964). [YML Yorkshire Pamphlets—SC-Pamph Box 147/14].

Other relevant studies

Hinchcliffe, Henry, *The Stained Glass Windows of Harry Stammers* (No location: Mindelph Press, 2016).

Riddick, Sarah, *Pioneer Studio Pottery: The Milner-White Collection*, ed. Richard Green (London: Lund Humphries and York City Art Gallery, 1990).

Warren, Allen, *Eric Milner-White: A Very English Anglo-Catholic, 1884–1963* (London: The Anglo-Catholic History Society Lecture, 2022).

Russell, Richard Squire, *Eric Milner-White Cleric and Collector*, 2004 (no place or publisher) [YML, SC, Yorkshire Pamphlets—SC-Pamph Box 143/4].

The Sheldon Memorial Trust, York, between 2010 and 2024 made recordings or conducted interviews with the very few of Milner's colleagues still alive at that time—including Henry Stapleton, Bernard Barr, Francis Jackson, and Peter Gibson. These can be consulted by contacting the secretary of the Trust at its website.

The *ODNB* entry was written by Dr Natalie K. Watson, presently the Publishing Director of Sacristy Press. The author would like to thank Dr Watson for her vigorous and constructive support in bringing this study forward for publication.

Personal Thanks

This volume and the seminar and lecture before it, would never have seen the light of day without the positive personal support of the late Sir Donald Barron and the late David Foster, one time Chairman of the Sheldon Memorial Trust, fellow colleagues on the lectures subcommittee of the Sheldon Memorial Trust. Sadly, two died in what has been a long journey. I hope they feel pleased with the result.

Among its members, Sarah Sheils [present Chair], Peter Addyman, Richard Green, Martin Picard, and the late Sir Donald Barron and David Foster, along with Professor Bill Sheils, brought their unique knowledge of the history of York to support the author, who is most grateful.

The author would like to thank Dr Patricia McGuire, Tom Davies, and all the King's College Archive Centre staff for their support for this project over the last five years. At York Minster Library and Archives, Natalie Toy, Steven Newman and Peter Young and their colleagues have been similarly interested and patient. Both Directors of the Borthwick Institute for Archives, Chris Webb and Gary Brannon as well as their colleagues have been continually helpful in challenging financial times in universities.

Paul Shields, the University of York's photographer, continues to be helpful to all, including long-retired members of the university's staff, including myself, who is profoundly grateful.

The author would also like to recognize the supportive generosity of Henry Hinchcliffe, pioneer champion of glass painter Harry Stammers, Milner-White's strongly preferred glass painter, for sanctioning the use of his text and images for which he holds the copyright.

My friend and former university colleague Professor Susan Mendus, FBA, a philosopher and in her words 'a lapsed Baptist', offered to both copy-edit an earlier version of the text, and to provide an external view about its interest and coherence to those interested in the many aspects of twentieth century English culture, religious and aesthetic, that Milner touched in a long Anglican priestly life. She also drew attention to my inconsistent use of the 'Oxford comma'!

My old friend the Revd Stephen Tucker, college contemporary, and later Chaplain of New College and Vicar of Hampstead, was a constructive presence throughout the project, as well as introducing me to the Society of the Faith. Their financial support for the aesthetic quality of the book's production would have been endorsed by its subject. To both I express the Sheldon Memorial Trust's deep appreciation.

Introduction

On Christmas Eve 1918, just six weeks after the Armistice, the newly elected Dean of King's College, Cambridge decided to hold a "Special Service" of Nine Lessons and Carols in the college's chapel. "Special" because 24 December is not recognized in the Book of Common Prayer and is outside "full" term in the university.[1] By implication, with no undergraduates present and only a few dons, it was a service for the citizens of Cambridge, beginning with a processional carol (originally *Hark! The Herald Angels Sing*, but almost immediately in succeeding years and universally *Once in Royal David's City*), with a boy treble singing the first verse and the choir and congregation gradually joining the later verses. This was followed by a bidding prayer composed and spoken by the dean.

It was not wholly original in structure. In this version, it was a mixture of well-known texts from the Old Testament following the biblical story from Adam and Eve to the birth of Christ, combined with familiar and not so familiar carols sung by the choir or by the whole congregation together. What was totally new was the "bidding" prayer composed by the dean in the preceding weeks, a prayer of liturgical poetry written entirely within the spirit of the 1662 Book of Common Prayer, but catching the moment, just after the war had ended. While the content in musical terms

---

[1] "Special Services": Broadly, services not included within the Book of Common Prayer, of which services that were devised for Christmas Eve are a good example. Milner, who promoted the idea, particularly at York Minster, wrote more generally about how such services should be considered in the late 1950s in "Special Services: A Liturgical Need", *York Quarterly: The Organ of the Archbishop*, New series 10, February 1959, pp. 8–10.

might vary over the next hundred years, this bidding prayer has been used continuously, locally, and globally.[2]

But who was this new Dean of King's College, Cambridge, beginning 45 years as dean of two of the most famous churches within the Anglican Communion, first in Cambridge until 1941, and subsequently as Dean of York, the leading cathedral of the Northern Province until 1963?

---

[2]   For an insightful chapter on the evolution and early versions of the King's service, and its spread across the English-speaking world, see Nicholas Nash, "'A Right Prelude to Christmas': A History of a Festival of Nine Lessons and Carols", in Jean Michel Massing and Nicolette Zeeman (eds), *King's College Chapel 1515–2015* (London: Harvey Miller Publishers, 2014), pp. 323–46; Erik Routley, *The English Carol* (London: H. Jenkins, 1958), pp. 248–9. For a more recent comment, see Benji Stegner, "For He Is Our Childhood's Pattern: A Festival of Nine Lessons and Carols as an Intergenerational Model", *The Choral Journal* 60:5 (December 2019), pp. 10–19.

1

Family background and early education, 1884–1903

Eric Milner-White was born on 23 April 1884 at Northwood, Cowes, Isle of Wight, as the first of four sons of Henry White (1854–1922) and Katherine Lucy Meeres (1857–90).

Not that this was Eric's baptismal name, which is recorded as Eric Milner White, with the hyphen only added by his father in 1894, making a double-barrelled surname, following the death of his first wife (Eric's mother) in 1890. Eric's full name therefore became Eric Milner Milner-White. A pedantic academic opening, perhaps, but it is introduced to make the point that his father was as sensitive to social discrimination as was his later clerical son. Henry White's family was already reasonably well-established on the island in the year of his own birth in 1854, based in the village of Northwood, just south of Cowes, with a prosperity derived from shipbuilding, corn milling and the law. Robert White (1818–62), Henry's father, described himself in 1861 as a "retired ship builder" aged 42.

The White family had prospered in the years after 1800 as Cowes became the premier established yachting centre in England, patronized by the Prince Regent, and the home of the Royal Yacht Squadron in 1815, its reputation enhanced by the building of a royal residence at Osborne in the late 1840s.

They were a pious family with a tendency towards high churchmanship. The youngest of their six children, Henry (Milner's father) was the third son of Robert and his wife, Louisa (1818–98), daughter of a local brewer. Franklin, the eldest son, has no recorded education, but became a mining engineer, married a Northwood girl, Susannah, in 1879, and had a son, also Franklin, in 1889. The middle son, Reginald, and his younger brother Henry were educated privately by their brother-in-law, the Revd Arthur Watson, who had married their sister, Caroline, in 1864. Himself the son of a cleric, Watson had gone up to Gonville and Caius College, Cambridge in 1854. Ordained deacon in 1862 and priested the following year, he became the headmaster of the Grange School in West Cowes two years later, a tenure that was to last until 1920.[1]

Henry followed his older brother to Pembroke College, Cambridge in 1874 to read law, graduating in 1878. It is likely that he returned to the Isle of Wight, as he married Katherine Lucy Meeres in June 1883. She was also from the island's professional classes, her father being a surgeon, with her family living at Egypt House, a large contemporary mansion on the sea front in West Cowes.

Eric (later always known outside his family as Milner), our subject, was Henry and Lucy's first child, born on St George's Day 1884. At the same time, his father joined the Inner Temple and was called to the Bar in 1886. It is not clear if he ever practised in London, although he was usually recorded as a barrister and later company director.

Much earlier, Henry's eldest sister Louisa (Fanny), who had become a governess, married Edwin Jones (1832–96) in 1869 as his second wife. Born into a humble family from Romsey in north Hampshire, Edwin Jones had made his way through the drapery business to become, by the time of his second marriage, a leading citizen in Southampton as the owner of its first department store, bearing his name. He was also a strong civic presence and was mayor of the town for two years in 1873 and 1875. It was an entrepreneurial story that could be seen across the UK in the second half of the century, with Joseph Chamberlain, from Birmingham, the most frequently quoted example, himself mayor of Birmingham in the same period. Jones had had a daughter by his first wife but no direct male heir, and his marriage to Louisa (Fanny) meant that Henry became Edwin's brother-in-law, in effect joining the "family firm". In 1888, Edwin Jones had become a limited company, but one in which all shares were owned by family or friends. With no obvious other

---

[1]   Family information from census data—drawn from Ancestry UK/National Archives.

male heir (Franklin was a mining engineer and Reginald an Anglican priest), Henry's succession seemed assured.[2]

In 1890, both families lived on the prosperous perimeters of Southampton in substantial late Victorian villas on either side of the Itchen. They were active citizens and committed members of the local Anglican church. Henry was president of the Southampton Chamber of Trade on three occasions, patron of sporting clubs, an active supporter of tariff reform and welfare societies. He was also committed to higher education and training in the town, and treasurer of Hartley College in Southampton from 1906, with its ambitions to become the town's university. He was also actively involved in diocesan church affairs, being secretary of the national Church Congress in the year that the Congress met in Southampton in 1913.

Following their marriage, Henry and his wife had had four sons—Eric, Rudolph, Norman, and Basil. They lived with Henry's widowed mother, a governess, nanny, cook, and other indoor servants. Their lifestyles were fully typical of the wealthy provincial haute bourgeoisie of the period, families living among the "vineries and pineries", in Lord Randolph Churchill's withering phrase.[3] But then tragedy struck the family: the two younger sons, Norman and Basil, and their mother died within six years, with only the two elder sons surviving.

Eric's father later married Annie Teasdale (1864–1951) as his second wife in 1895, the only child of Robert Teasdale JP (1809–83), of Cockerton, near Darlington. At one level, the White family of the Isle of Wight and the Teasdales from the North-East could not have been more different in location, work (shipbuilding and provincial industrial finance) and religion (high church Anglicans and deeply committed Free Methodists), but at others they were similar in being provincial, industrious, and ambitious socially, financially, and civically, especially in terms of education and training. Neither had any desire to become "gentlemen" through the purchase of a landed country estate. They

---

2   For Edwin Jones, see *Southampton Observer and Hampshire News*, 1 August 1896, p. 6.

3   Winston Spencer Churchill, MP, *Lord Randolph Churchill*, Vol. 1 (London: Macmillan, 1905), p. 345.

lived comfortable, responsible, bourgeois lives on the rural perimeters of the urban centres, which had provided the environment for their own betterment.

Eric had little memory of his own mother, always seeing his stepmother as his mother. This is hardly surprising, given that his natural mother had died when he was five, and during his early years she had had three later pregnancies. What is recorded is that Milner did admire his new mother's care of his youngest brother's illness and death. Their relationship remained close throughout her long life, especially after her widowhood in 1922, with Milner's younger surviving brother, Rudolph, having joined the judicial branch of the Indian Civil Service in 1909.[4]

In 1894, on his father's remarriage, the new family moved into a larger house, Deepdene, in the nearby parish of Bitterne. Milner (as we will now call him) was ten, already at school locally, firstly at a "kindergarten" and then at Highfield, later a well-known proprietorial preparatory school at Liphook, where it remains. But, at this time, it was simply a local school in Southampton, near to the Milner-Whites' home, taking largely day pupils in small numbers. For a widowed father with young sons, it was ideal. Milner seems to have enjoyed it. Its founding proprietary head, Mr M. R. Wells, also had ambitions for his pupils to move on to major English public boarding schools, which Milner duly did, to Harrow in 1897.

The Harrow School archives record little about Milner's time at the school. The historian depends on the Wilkinson tribute in 1963, itself probably based on earlier conversations with Milner at King's in the late 1930s.[5] From this we learn that he was in Moreton's House under house master Colbeck, an able boy as well as a good sportsman. He became head of his house early and may have been bullied in the athletic philistinism of the late Victorian public school. In this respect, Harrow, as one of the great nine "Clarendon" schools, was not unrepresentative, but it had one or two distinctive features. As its historian, Professor Christopher Tyerman, himself an "old boy", notes, Harrow was not a rich

---

[4]   Rudolph Milner-White (1885–1954), Harrow and Pembroke College (m. 1905).

[5]   Wilkinson, *Milner-White*, pp. 6–7.

school in comparison to its peers, Eton and Winchester, nor did it have a sister college at Cambridge or Oxford (King's College and New College) or close connections with the Crown or the late medieval Church. It was not especially pious. This resulted in a clientele of traditional aristocratic, landed families, and "newish" money from those who had recently done well in manufacturing, trade, and finance, often in the provinces. Henry Milner-White was not untypical in sending both Milner and his younger brother, Rudolph, to the school.[6]

Slightly misleadingly, Wilkinson records that Milner saw Townsend Warner as the master who influenced him the most by developing his ability to write English. In fact, Warner was the head of history at the school as well as a Fellow of Jesus College, Cambridge, and a prolific writer for schools on historical topics, including also a guide on "How to write English". We must presume that he had some influence in Milner's decision to study history at Cambridge, where he won an open scholarship to King's College in 1903. This was achieved on the back of school prizes and a status within the school. As a result, he was invited in 1905 to join his younger brother in taking a lead in some of the dramatic performances staged at Harrow during the visit of Edward VII and Queen Alexandra in the autumn of that year.[7] Milner had made one significant friend at Harrow in Gerald Fitzgerald, son of a lawyer and probably a friend of his father through the law. Fitzgerald also secured a place at King's to read history, later becoming a lawyer himself, before being killed as Captain Fitzgerald near Armentières in December 1915. One of the new and later windows in King's Chapel, created by Milner himself from medieval fragments, is dedicated to his oldest friend.[8]

---

[6]   Christopher Tyerman, *A History of Harrow School, 1324–1991* (Oxford: Clarendon Press, 2000), pp. 355–402.

[7]   "Shakespeare's *Henry VI* and Aristophanes' *The Frogs*". Report on the royal visit, *Hampshire Advertiser*, 8 July 1905, p. 12.

[8]   Wilkinson, *Milner-White*, p. 7. It is worth noting that Milner was a loyal, if not passionate, Old Harrovian, unlike his idealizing of King's College, Cambridge. Also interesting is that neither Harrow nor King's benefitted from personal gifts during his lifetime or later from his will.

2

King's College, Cambridge, 1903–7[1]

Milner's success in the competitive entry to King's turned out to be one
of the most significant moments of his life. Both his father and uncle had
gone to Pembroke College, as did his younger brother in 1904, so it seems
likely that the same plan had been anticipated for Milner. But, as we shall
see, King's College, Cambridge in 1903 was a very distinctive institution.
It began a life-long affair for Milner until his death in 1963, with three

---

[1] The main printed sources for the history of King's since 1870 are the writings
of L. P. Wilkinson, published by the Provost and Fellows of King's. These
included brief memorial tributes to prominent Fellows, including that to
Milner-White, cited in the introduction, published lists of Kingsmen, and a
pair of interpretative studies arising from that detailed work: L. P. Wilkinson,
Kingsmen of a Century, 1873–1972 (Cambridge: King's College, repr. with
corrections 1981); *A Century of King's, 1873–1972* (Cambridge: King's
College, 1980). On Wilkinson, see Donald Parry, *Lancelot Patrick Wilkinson,
1907–1985, fellow, tutor and Vice Provost, lecturer in classics* (Cambridge:
King's College, 1985). An important source for the domestic tone of the
college from 1900 until the late 1930s is the undergraduate publication
Basileon, its title translated as "King of Kings". Before 1914, its flavour was
artistic and literary, with contributions from E. M. Forster, Rupert Brooke,
Stephen Gaselee, and H. O. Meredith. After 1918, it shifted towards humour
and benign satire, with Milner as dean a regular butt of the undergraduate
attention. In the later 1920s, L. P. Wilkinson was himself a regular contributor
as an undergraduate. A facsimile of the magazine for the pre-1914 period
was published by Sir Charles Tennyson (ed.), *Basileon 1900–14: Magazine
of King's College, Cambridge,* facsimile with intro. 1974. The originals are in
the King's College Archive Centre under College Archives—*Basileon.*

of the priests officiating at his memorial service in York Minster being Kingsmen.[2] What was, therefore, so distinctive about the collegial life at King's in this period, and how did it impact on a young man described by Wilkinson as "tall, good looking . . . with dark hair, parted in the middle and a moustache, full of yest and ideas for entertainment . . ."?[3]

King's College, Cambridge and its chapel are, of course, one of the iconic sets of buildings and gardens in western Europe and around the world. A joint foundation with Eton by Henry VI in the mid-fifteenth century, the two colleges had remained indissolubly linked until the mid-nineteenth century. From the mid-1850s, however, the combination of statutory reforms of Oxford and Cambridge and changes in opinion about university education in general had prompted debates among the colleges and the university. The outcomes varied considerably. The changes after 1873 were substantial, seeing two conjoined colleges with introverted historic structures becoming, in the case of King's, a leading and wholly independent intellectual, scholarly, and sporting institution, with competitive entry drawing from a limited range of leading schools. In this evolution, it had cultivated a self-image of being a very informal, liberal, and creative place of learning, not large in numbers (150 undergraduates in total) or especially aristocratic, preparing its students for careers in the professions. King's and its larger and wealthier aristocratic neighbours, Trinity and St John's, saw themselves as in the top division, each with a very "special" atmosphere, or as Milner put it at the end of his time as a Life Fellow of King's, "this blessed place".[4]

It is very difficult to capture the atmosphere and impact of such an environment on the transitory and varied cohorts of undergraduate students, especially if they leave no memoirs. In trying to describe the undergraduate atmosphere of King's in its variety at that period, two

---

2   Pare and Harris, *Milner-White: A Memoir*, p. 91.

3   Wilkinson, *Milner-White*, p. 7.

4   "This blessed place"—private information. For the history of King's from 1850, see Wilkinson and his other writings above, n1. Also C. R. Fay, *King's College, Cambridge* (1907). No publisher named.

elements seem to have been part of the formative mix that fashioned Milner's character and subsequent career.

The first is suggested in the *Bildungsroman* of Sir Shane Leslie, who wrote three novels centred on his own experiences of Eton and King's before 1914 (but written post-war). The second novel of *The Cantab* (1926) is constructed around a naïve young man from a clerical background coming up to Cambridge and his "life story" until 1914, involving faith, doubt, catholic influences, urban mission, sexual awakening, temptation, and resolution. Leslie, from an Anglo-Irish background and a cousin of Winston Churchill, had come up to read classics at King's in 1906, but only took Part 1 of the Tripos in 1907, before transferring to the Sorbonne, and converting to Roman Catholicism in 1908. Not great literature, nor the only example of the genre, it possibly owes something to the first part of Compton Mackenzie's *Sinister Street* (1913). The reader will make what they will of it, but it does bring together many of the elements within the collegiate atmosphere of King's of the period.[5]

The second, and very different, element is that of the secret society, the Apostles, whose membership was dominated by the three "grand" colleges mentioned earlier, and for whom the principal mentor was the young philosopher G. E. Moore, a Fellow of Trinity, whose *Principia Ethica* was first published in October 1903, the month that Milner went up to King's.

The Apostles have dominated much of the later general writing about the University of Cambridge before 1914. Founded as a secret society in 1820, its membership of dons and undergraduates included, after 1900, Henry Sidgwick, G. E. Moore, Maynard Keynes, Rupert Brooke, Lytton Strachey, and Leonard Woolf. As a self-consciously elitist intellectual and artistic group, they feature prominently in the historiography, largely because of their later involvement with the Bloomsbury Group of artists and writers dominated by Leonard and Virginia Woolf. As young men at Cambridge, they had come together through the intra-connected world of their schools and colleges. They saw themselves as liberal in personal

---

5   Sir Justin Randolf [Shane] Leslie (1885–1971), *ODNB*, vol. 33, pp. 464–6. *The Cantab* (London: Chatto & Windus, 1926).

values, modernists in arts and literature, and as agnostic or atheist in religion.[6]

At first glance, Milner might seem from Wilkinson's earlier description to have been an ideal candidate for the Apostles—able, sporting, and handsome. Nor did his academic performance dint those impressions—a double first in the history Tripos and the winning of one of the leading competitive scholarships in the university, the Lightfoot Scholarship in ecclesiastical history, in 1906.

But this did not happen, which makes the point that over-attention to the Apostles distorts our general view of the Cambridge of the period. If there was a principal quality that united the Apostles, it was their agnosticism or atheism. More than anything else, this separates the Apostles from Milner and other more representative Kingsmen of his generation.

At King's, Wilkinson makes it clear that the Fellows and the governing body were also divided on religious issues, with both sceptical and liberal Christians represented. These differences spilled over into the undergraduate mind in the atmosphere of informal familiarity that was part of the college's self-image.

A single example from 1903 will have to suffice. The late Victorian period was marked by new patterns of social mission among the privileged classes to have an impact on the conditions of life in many working-class urban areas. Alongside the growth of uniformed youth movements, moral leagues such as the Band of Hope, and patriotic and imperial bodies like those encouraging the celebration of Empire Day, was the Settlement movement. This often took the form in schools and universities of members and immediate past members living in the poorest urban areas, providing a whole range of education, welfare, rescue, and employment services of which Toynbee Hall in Whitechapel (founded

---

6   On the Apostles, see W. E. Lubenow, *The Cambridge Apostles, 1820–1914* (Cambridge: University Press, 1999); Paul Levy, *G. E. Moore and the Cambridge Apostles* (London: Weidenfeld & Nicolson, c.1980). On the intellectual atmosphere at this period, the Royal Economic Society, *The Collected Writings of John Maynard Keynes, X. Essays in Biography, My Early Beliefs* (London: Royal Economic Society, 1972), pp. 433–51.

1884) is the first and the most famous example. Oxbridge colleges and public schools were particularly prominent, leading Trinity, St John's, and Gonville and Caius from Cambridge to found settlements in the newly created diocese of Southwark, which was already acquiring its radical social image. At King's, the college Fellows and undergraduates debated whether it should do the same, given that many of those volunteering were intending Anglican ordinands. In early 1903, the governing body decided against, as did the undergraduates in their own poll, each favouring a less obviously Christian initiative in Barnwell, a poor area north-east of Cambridge.[7]

Milner shared little of the sceptical agnosticism of the Apostles. He remained firmly within the high church Anglicanism of his family in Southampton, little influenced by the athletic hedonism of his old school. With Oxford and Cambridge supplying so many prospective ordinands, it is not surprising that the largest Cambridge undergraduate society throughout these years was the reinvigorated Christian Society.[8]

In his first two years, Milner seems to have thrown himself expansively into general undergraduate life, continuing to play sport, to be active in the pre-eminent society in the college, the Political Society, founded in 1880 and presided over by his tutor, Oscar Browning, and to spread his wings. He also became a member of small clubs by election, some secretive, a feature of college life of the period. Many of these clubs, including the Apostles, had overlapping memberships. Throughout his adult life, Milner was attracted to small, self-selecting clubs and societies, through which informal influence could be exercised, a trait that led to him later being seen as scheming by some.

In Milner's case, the most important college undergraduate club were the Trappists, a secret quasi-religious gathering, with members using fantastical literary names of a Gothic, Gaelic and classical pedigree, and whose papers and minutes remained among Milner's few surviving personal documents at his death in 1963. They wore distinctive robes,

---

[7]   Barnwell, Newmarket Road, Cambridge, dominated at this time by its housing for local brick and railway workers.

[8]   Alan Pigott, *An educated sense of fitness: Liberal Anglo-Catholicism, 1900–1940* (University of Oxford, DPhil, 2002).

debated a Rule for themselves, and came together in their rooms in silence, sacramentally circulating and drinking from a bowl of cows' milk, before speaking and debating. Milner himself used the name of Ulfilas/ Ulphilas (c.311–83), a Goth missionary and bishop at the time of the Arian controversy, recognized as leading the translation of the Bible into Gothic. As a college society, it lasted barely three years, reflecting the year of admission of most of its members (1903). Although adopting secret names and titles for themselves, we can identify reasonably confidently some of its members (never more than eight to ten) as including Will Spens (1901), possibly the founder, taking the name Merlin, Stephen Gaselee (1901), Charles Stanley Phillips (1902), Alwyn Faber Schofield (1903), Richard Fitzroy Barley (1903), Alfred Dillwyn Knox (1903), Philip Loyd (1903), William Douglas Hill (1903) and Milner himself. The fact that Milner quickly became a member, and came to hold its archives throughout his life, indicates its importance to him.

It is likely that Milner's earliest and closest friends at Cambridge were drawn from this "fraternity".[9] By the beginning of Milner's third

---

9   The five closest of Milner's friends as recorded by Wilkinson, including Gerald Fitzgerald, were Will Spens, Philip Loyd and Douglas Hill, all of whom were probably Trappists. Arthur Edghill was also included, although there is no evidence that he was a Trappist. Philip Loyd (1884–1952) was more important than any other, and acknowledged by Milner himself as the person who led him to understand the "sacramental" nature of his faith. An Etonian, and from the prominent private banking family of Samuel Loyd, he was also very able, reading classics, and from an Eton house that had also included Julian Huxley and Ronald Knox. He secured first-class honours at the same time as deciding on ordination. Although Loyd and Milner were exact undergraduate contemporaries, Loyd entered Cuddesdon in 1909, after an extended period of European travel, at times with his elder brother Lewis. Ordained priest in 1911, he served initially at the Eton College mission in Hackney Wick (1910–12), joining Milner in his own sabbatical from his curacy in Woolwich during 1909–10. In 1912, Loyd was appointed as Vice-Principal of Cuddesdon, before moving to India in 1915 as a mission priest in the Bombay diocese. Consecrated as the founding bishop of the new diocese of Nasik, north of Mumbai, in 1929, he returned to the UK in 1944 to become

year (1905), some of these relationships had become personally and religiously intense. Hill, also educated at Harrow, had written to Milner in the previous long vacation that he should take himself more seriously and less frivolously. Milner was deeply hurt, so much so that he experienced what might be called a "Damascene moment", which he recorded in some detail in his commonplace book. The episode lasted several days, during which Milner had physical symptoms of intense sweating, fear of being left alone, and a "vision" of Christ walking among a group of city street boys. From that point, Milner knew that he wished to be a priest.[10]

This "crisis" involved complex religious, personal, and moral anxieties centred on faith, belief, and personal integrity, not itself unusual among groups of able, earnest young men. He described the episode as "frightening".

There may be another element linked to Milner's later increasingly aesthetic personality and his concern for "beauty" in the decorative arts, combined with his own style and tone of writing and speaking, elements which were later commonly seen as precious. It seems that these artistic and aesthetic interests developed alongside the more routine

---

the Bishop of St Albans until two years before his death in 1952. Unmarried, he shared Milner's Anglo-Catholic sentiments. R. P. Stacey Waddy, *Philip Loyd: Missionary and Bishop* (London: Mowbray's, 1954). William Douglas Hill (1884–1962), son of a successful London accountant and actuary, living in Kensington, was also educated at Harrow and by 1911 was a master at Eton. Later he became a Church Missionary Society evangelist in India (1918–28). Remembered as a serious young man, he was already interested in eastern religions, making one of the earlier and more definitive translations of the Bhagavad-Gita, published by the Oxford University Press in 1928. He later became the Principal of the Narayan High School in Benares until he retired. He died in Poole, Dorset in 1962. William Spens (1882–1962): *ODNB*, vol. 51, pp. 916–18.

10   For Milner's personal crisis, see KCAC, Modern Archives, GBR/0272/EMW/2/16, including introspective notes on his own unworthiness. Simultaneously, he was reading Richard Baxter, *The Saints Everlasting Rest* (1650). Baxter was the nominated churchman on whom candidates entering for the Lightfoot Scholarship, 1905–6, had to study and write.

undergraduate concerns relating to academic progress, sport, and a future career. We know that this period also marks Milner's early interest in opera, attending Covent Garden, often alone, and hearing Caruso, McCormack, Melba and Wittich among others, usually conducted by Hans Richter. This experience was extended in 1910 when, on leave in Europe owing to having mysteriously lost his voice, he and probably Loyd visited cathedral cities and the local opera houses, before attending the Passion Play in Oberammergau.[11]

A glimpse of Milner at this early stage of his Cambridge life is provided by an anonymous comment by the head Trappist in the club's minutes that Milner "wishes to aspire, and does not mind the consequential fall. As a brother he has a very good opinion of himself."[12]

This entry into artistic circles was probably stimulated by the personality and public reputation of his tutor, Oscar Browning, with his connections to another aesthetic group, presided over by the scholarly university librarian, Charles Sayle. Sayle's circle of librarians and bibliophiles were interested in medieval manuscripts, early printed books, and the associated decorative arts. They gathered at his "salon" in the Trumpington Road with its strongly homoerotic atmosphere, with members including Rupert Brooke, George Mallory, Cosmo Gordon, Stephen Gaselee, Maynard Keynes and his brother Geoffrey, and possibly Milner himself. Many of the same young men were also members of the Baskerville Club founded in 1903 by Sayle, also dedicated to manuscripts and bibliography.[13] Sayle was certainly attracted by the friendship of handsome young men, as A. C. Benson's extensive diaries show. Benson

---

[11] For Milner's operatic interests, see The Brotherton Library, University of Leeds, Special Collections, Music A-O-05 WHI—preserved opera programmes 1905–14.

[12] KCAC/Modern Archives/GBR/0272/EMW/2/1–2.

[13] The Baskerville Club, founded by Sayle in October 1903 to encourage bibliographical studies, included Maynard Keynes and Stephen Gaselee (both King's) among its founding members, and had Geoffrey Keynes among its later active members. See Cambridge University Library, CUL, GBR/0012/MS Add 6673.

himself had already noticed Milner, when attending evensong in King's College Chapel, at which Milner was reading a lesson as a scholar.[14]

It is interesting that Wilkinson chose, perhaps unsurprisingly, to make no reference at all to Oscar Browning in his own tribute to Milner, commissioned and published by the Provost and Fellows of King's, just six months after his death in 1963. Even 50 years later, Browning was still a college figure arousing strong opinions. This is to be contrasted with Wilkinson's final volume devoted to recent King's history, *A Century of King's Men, 1872 to 1972*, published in 1980, in which Browning features prominently as one of the more colourful, if controversial, college personalities of the late Victorian period.[15]

The suggestion that Milner may have become familiar with the circle around Charles Sayle comes from the privately published *Letters of Hugh Stanley Wilson*, who was killed on 14 September 1915 at Hébuterne on the Pas-de-Calais. The evidence is circumstantial, if plausible. A contemporary of Milner as an undergraduate at King's, Wilson (1904–7), son of a canon of Worcester, educated at Clifton, was an assistant master at Rugby in 1914. The memorial collection of his letters to family and friends (1920) has no editors on the spine but was finely printed on high-quality paper and bound with attractive boards. It was in fact brought together by two other King's men of that generation, Geoffrey Keynes, later a distinguished doctor and literary scholar, brother of Maynard, and Cosmo Gordon (also a keen bibliographer at that time), both of whom were members of the Baskerville Club and part of the Sayle fraternity in the years 1903 to 1907. The publication of the letters was put together with the active collaboration of Wilson's family, with many being from Wilson to Sayle. None are by Milner himself, but his own copy of the volume is in York Minster Library, including his personal book plate in the style of Eric Gill. It was published privately, shortly after he had become dean.[16]

---

[14]   David Newsome, *On the Edge of Paradise: A. C. Benson, the Diarist* (London: John Murray, 1996), entry p. 183, no date, probably 1905.

[15]   Wilkinson, see Chapter 2, footnote 1 above.

[16]   Anon. (Geoffrey Keynes and Cosmo Gordon), *Letters of Hugh Stanley Wilson to his family and friends* (Cambridge: King's College, Cambridge, privately

For Milner, active in many parts of collegial undergraduate life, encouraged by academic success and preparing for the Lightfoot Scholarship examinations, criticism about his behaviour towards his friends brought on the turmoil and personal crisis. The fact of his recording that moment in detail, and that he returned to it in the mid-1920s, similarly recorded and not later destroyed, is perhaps some indication of its importance. From about this moment, his journey towards ordination was clear.

But critical as this crisis was in Milner's early development, it must not detract from his academic progress as a very successful history undergraduate. History had only been a single subject honours degree at Cambridge since the 1870s. Of the colleges offering it, King's was significantly the most successful of the trio of Trinity, St John's and King's.[17] This reintroduces a new "character" in the figure of Oscar Browning (1837–1923), probably the best-known Cambridge don among the educated public at the time.[18] Himself a product of Eton and King's, he had returned to the school in 1860, becoming a very successful and well-paid housemaster, popular with boys and parents alike. From the outset, he had been a challenging figure in a deeply conservative institution, famously dismissed by the headmaster in 1875 after colleagues' complaints about his innovative style of teaching and house-mastering, combined with his close relations with selected pupils, the most famous of whom was the young George Nathaniel Curzon. Consequently, Browning had to fall back on his much less well-remunerated Fellowship at King's and as a lecturer in history.[19]

In 1903, Browning was aged 66 and coming to the end of his career, but over the previous 20 years had become a Cambridge phenomenon as well as a very successful teacher and inspirer of the young, if less popular

---

printed, 1919), Wilson MSS, KCAC/Modern Manuscripts/GBR/0272/HSW.

[17]   For history success, see Browning's letter to *Basileon* in June 1919, noting that in the first 22 years following the establishment of the History Tripos up to 1906, King's had secured 45 firsts, Trinity 30 and St John's 16. Browning had retired in 1909.

[18]   Oscar Browning (1837–1923), *ODNB*, vol. 8, pp. 249–51.

[19]   Oscar Browning (1837–1923), *ODNB*, vol. 8, p. 249.

with many of the dons. For much of the twentieth century, Browning has been presented either as an egotistical misogynistic snob or part of that generation that included William Johnson (Cory), Browning's own tutor at Eton, and Oscar Wilde, who Browning knew and supported, which is part of the "gay" story. More recently, his Cambridge career has been treated more generously, drawing attention to his role in the founding of the Royal Historical Society, including publishing papers in the early volumes of its *Transactions*, and his pioneering work on teachers' training along with the university extension movement.[20] His innovative, and very personal, style of teaching gives him some claim to be the founder of the academic seminar in English universities. Among many other connections, his friendship with George Eliot and his respected study of the novelist adds a dimension to his "character". He was a privileged radical in politics, unsuccessfully contesting a parliamentary election on three occasions, a supporter of women's suffrage and engaged with other cultures and faiths. His enormous personal archive has the potential to form an essay in late nineteenth- and early twentieth-century cultural history alone.[21]

This was the man who awarded Milner an open scholarship, just after he had returned from India, following a five-week tour in some luxury as the guest of his old Eton pupil, George Nathaniel Curzon, now Viceroy. Milner and Browning got on well. Even before going up, Milner was writing on his own and Gerald Fitzgerald's behalf for pre-term reading. That correspondence was sustained up to 1914, some years after Browning had retired to Bexhill. It is one of the very few collections of personal letters written by Milner that have survived (in Browning's own papers and so escaping the later pruning). Almost from the start, they adopted a skittish, almost flirtatious, conversational style, which both clearly enjoyed. They provide not only a commentary by Milner on his undergraduate years, but also a picture of Browning's teaching method, which was largely conducted through the proceedings of the College Political Society, which Browning had established in 1880

---

[20]   Oscar Browning, "The Teaching of History in Schools", *Transactions of the Royal Historical Society* (New Second Series), vol. IV (1889), pp. 69–84.

[21]   KCAC/Modern Archives/GBR/0272/OB.

on appointment. Presiding in his own set of rooms, lavishly furnished, meetings were a combination of "salon" and debating club. It seems likely that membership was by invitation, and did not include all those studying history. Usually, an undergraduate gave a paper on a political or historical topic, which was discussed and debated, following which there was a division on a motion, relating to but not determined strictly by the paper presented. Given that Browning believed that a King's education was a training for future statesmanship, it was not a bad preparation for that calling. The minute book of the society, of which Milner was secretary in his third year, survives and gives a context and depth to his personal letters.[22]

This is particularly helpful in relation to Milner as, after his decision to become a priest, we know almost nothing of his general opinions about contemporary politics and society in Britain or in any other European or imperial context, both before and after the Great War. For example, there is nothing in his later sermons in south London from 1908 until 1912 to show if the local social conditions had any impact on his general views on politics, society, or religion. This was despite the major industrial strife during 1911 in London and elsewhere, with Will Crooks, probably the most well-known radical politician in London at the time, being Milner's local MP for Woolwich.

So how can we describe the clever, young historian's opinions in mid-1906, at least as measured by his votes at the Political Society? Perhaps not surprisingly, he was hostile to trade unions and to municipal socialism, and retrospectively still supported the South in the American Civil War. He did not think highly of Wolsey, Charles James Fox, Disraeli, or Parnell; he supported the separation of religion and politics, and did not agree that history is "a science, no more, no less".[23] He did not

---

22   For the Political Society minute book, KCAC/College Archives/GBR/0272/ KCAS/Political Society. Milner was secretary in his third year and gave papers himself on "the Indian Frontier and Beyond" (24 October 1904), "the Tudor Sea Venturers" (20 October 1905) and "General Booth as a modern St Francis" (2 November 1907).

23   J. B. Bury's inaugural as Regius Professor in early 1903 and Charles Firth's inaugural as Regius Professor in Oxford in November 1904 were both in

believe that the Reformation changed the "character" of the English, he was positive about imperial federation but did not support tariff reform (unlike his father), and on three occasions voted against respect for Islam. Do these division records show anything more than an undergraduate debating vote? Perhaps not too much. But one or two features might seem indicative. Broadly, he was an intelligent young Englishman, with the moderately conservative opinions of his class and successful provincial business background, but in his case, more unusually, from a pious family with a strong commitment to high church Anglicanism. It is interesting that he had a low opinion of Disraeli. He clearly expresses more than once that he saw "nationality" as one of the driving forces in history, as indicated in his view about the impact of the Reformation. It is also intriguing that he thought that religion should be separated from politics.

It may be that in these votes, we see the beginnings of the cleric, who was a historian in the narrative mode of his tutor, rather than an academic philosopher, theologian, or "scientific" historian, fashioning the elements of an ecclesiology anchored in his family's high churchmanship. By the 1920s, these were expressed as a distinctive (but not wholly original), historically organic English tradition of Christian practice and doctrine, parallel and equal to those of the Roman Church and that of the Eastern Orthodox. In this interpretation, firstly, the Reformation (called the Renaissance in England in Milner's university lectures in the 1920s) was a critical developmental episode, but one which had not altered the

---

a similar vein, with Firth's entitled "A Plea for the Historical Teaching of History". Both lectures challenged the existing manner of collegiate teaching of history as reflected in both Browning's style and that of F. F. Urquhart at Balliol College, Oxford, each with a powerful influence at that time. Francis Fortescue Urquhart (1868–1934), *ODNB*, vol. 55, pp. 948–9, for example, in a long career as Dean and Fellow in History at Balliol College, was an important influence on the young Harold Macmillan before 1914, and on A. J. P. Taylor in the late 1920s (private information). KCAC Political Society Minute Book, 20 November 1906, in which Milner voted against Bury's claim in a majority of 10–2, including both Browning and Spens.

"English character".[24] What could not be contradicted was that it had changed the relations between Church and State in England. Secondly, his attitude to other faiths, especially "Hindooism", and even Islam ("a Judaic faith"), is very alien to today's reader, but not wholly untypical of the age.[25]

There is an additional element to Milner's individual scholarly development, which becomes an important aspect of his Anglican ecclesiology: the award of the Lightfoot university scholarship. This involved examinations on Church history and a research project nominated by the examiners on an annual basis. For the academic year 1905 to 1906, it was the controversial Puritan Richard Baxter (1615–91). It is quite likely that Milner, aged 21, was not widely read in sixteenth- and seventeenth-century Anglican writing as the context to his understanding of Baxter, including Cranmer, Hooker, Lancelot Andrewes, and Laud. His immersion in these subjects may have been something of a "crash course". He read hard for the examinations, with these writers becoming central to his ecclesiology and his catholic view of Anglicanism. This centrally involved the concept of the "via media" as expressed by Richard Hooker in his *Laws of Ecclesiastical Polity* of 1594–7.[26]

In terms of the literary and religious culture of the period, Milner had also become aware of two important discoveries in the years before his ordination. The first was the poetry of the seventeenth-century divine Thomas Traherne, whose lost works were being discovered for the first time in the 1890s, of which Milner's favourite, *Centuries of Meditations*,

---

24 Reformation and English character—KCAC/Political Society Minute Book, 25 February 1907.

25 Milner's votes are recorded in the minutes of the Political Society, KCAC/ Political Society Minute Book. See also Milner-White's review in *London Bridge* (the house journal of St Saviour's College, Southwark), 4 January 1911, p. 253, on the choice facing Christian missionaries in India of how they should approach their work, as between using the caste system or conversion directly, KCAC, Modern Archives, GBR/0272/EMW/4/4/1.

26 Lightfoot Scholarship—a one-year scholarship awarded (today) by the history faculty as an essay on ecclesiastical history in memory of J. B. Lightfoot (1828–89), Bishop of Durham, *ODNB*, Vol. 33, p. 757.

was edited and first published in 1908. A reading of these provides a window into Milner's developing spiritual personality and language. The second centred on the religious community of Little Gidding (1626–37) its inspirational founder, Nicholas Ferrar (1592–1637), and his Huntingdonshire family. Milner is reported as researching this topic in his two years as chaplain of King's between 1912 and 1914. His understanding of this self-defining and regulating Christian community influenced the thinking and "vision" he provided (as John How called it) for the early years of the Oratory of the Good Shepherd, before and after the Great War.[27]

---

[27] Henry R. T. Brandreth, *A History of the Oratory of the Good Shepherd: An Historical Sketch* (Cambridge: The Oratory of the Good Shepherd, 1958); George Tibbatts, *The Oratory of the Good Shepherd: The First Seventy-Five Years* (Windsor: The Almoner, Oratory of the Good Shepherd, 1988).

3

Cuddesdon, 1907–8

This was the ordinand who went to Cuddesdon in the autumn of 1907. As with King's, it was an institution that was to capture his life-long affections, with Milner reporting that he saw that his earlier opinions "received their form and order" during that year, and his interest in liturgy germinated.[1] This period is poorly covered in Cuddesdon's history, but it was and remains the Anglican theological college most closely associated with the moderate Anglo-Catholic tradition, dating from its founding by Bishop Samuel Wilberforce of Oxford in 1853 and its first vice-principal H. P. Liddon (1854–9). Although only resident for a year, Milner remained in close contact, certainly until he left Cambridge in 1941. He was also the most persuasive of deans in encouraging intending King's ordinands to choose Cuddesdon, so that it was claimed that on occasion 50 per cent of its Cambridge ordinands had come from King's. In part, this was because of his friendship with the principal, Eric Graham (1888–1964), later Bishop of Brechin (1944–59).[2] If any additional evidence is needed, it is in the *Cuddesdon Office Book* (1940), published by Oxford University Press, the result of nearly ten years of careful revision by Milner of previous versions, building on the original compiled by Liddon. A manual of Anglican worship throughout the Christian year of antiphons, readings, and prayers, it had been frequently amended and revised up to 1929.

---

[1] Wilkinson, *Milner-White*, pp. 8–9; Pare and Harris, *Milner-White: A Memoir*, pp. 10–12.

[2] Robert T. Holtby, *Eric Graham, 1888–1964* (Oxford: Clarendon Press, 1967).

In correspondence with the principal, Milner produced a definitive, amended, and supplemented edition over the following decade.[3]

So how should we characterize the young man ordained deacon in Southwark Cathedral in September 1908, joining the team of clergy attached to St Paul's, Lorrimore Square, a short distance from St Saviour's parish church, the choice as the new cathedral?

Summation

Son of a high church Southampton lawyer and successful businessman, who had become one of the town's leading citizens, Milner had received the typical education of the wealthy haute bourgeoisie at Harrow, before unexpectedly going to King's College, Cambridge on a scholarship to read history. He had done well academically, winning first-class honours and the Lightfoot Scholarship. A keen sportsman, especially cricket, he actively engaged in the affairs of the Political Society, coming under the influence of his tutor, one of the most well-known dons of the period, Oscar Browning, and his wider social and intellectual circle. These may have included those touched by the aesthetic homoerotic elements in the Cambridge of the period, including C. A. Sayle and the Uranian poets. Not tempted by the sceptical world of the Apostles, he was closely involved in a quasi-religious college group, the Trappists, undergoing a spiritual crisis in October 1905 which itself led directly to his decision to be ordained. The experience of the years at King's and Cuddesdon was formative, as is conveyed by comparing the two contemporary photos of Milner as a schoolboy and as a young priest five years later.

---

[3]   *Cuddesdon Office Book* (no identified editors, Oxford: Clarendon Press, 1940).

4

The young Anglo-Catholic
priest: Southwark, 1908–12

The diocese of Southwark, only created in 1905, covered probably the most
impoverished districts of south London and was the focus, along with
the East End, of the missions and settlements that proliferated in the city
and elsewhere following the founding of Toynbee Hall in 1884. Churches,
Oxbridge colleges, and public schools were all variously energetic in their
"mission" to the poor. As with the later role of chaplains in the Great
War, there has been considerable revisionism in the historiography over
the last 40 years about the impact of the settlement movement in poor
districts in London and other cities. In the 1960s and beyond, those
involved in Christian social mission among the urban poor were often
treated by historians as marginal to the wider questions of religion,
class, secularization, and politics. That has changed considerably, and
in the case of Southwark through an impressive study by S. C. Williams
(1999) in which she subtly and thoroughly explores the social evidence to
reveal the complex social, religious and cultural history of the area.[1] The
Fellows of King's, along with its undergraduates, had declined to sanction
their own settlement in London because they feared it would have a too
Christian ethos, agreeing to work on social mission in Barnwell in north
Cambridge. This ignored the fact that these settlements were centres of
a whole range of activities—religious, educational, rescue, sporting and
social—as any study of the *Toynbee Record* testifies, among many others.
Anglo-Catholic parishes have rightly taken pride in their working-class

---

[1]   S. C. Williams, *Religious Belief and Popular Culture in Southwark 1880–1939*
(Oxford: Clarendon Press, 1999).

commitment. But other denominations take similar, if less well-known, pride—for instance, that of the Methodist missions in the City of London. St Paul's, Lorrimore Square, close to St Saviour's, Southwark, to which Milner was attached as a deacon, is a case in point. It was a parish that had taken earlier high church ordinands from Cambridge and was in the middle of one of the poorest areas south of the river.[2] Led by the Revd Arthur Milner Pickering, it was a recognized Anglo-Catholic parish with the full calendar of services throughout the Christian year, a mission church, with guilds, clubs, and societies. Pickering (Eton and Clare), from a substantial North Riding of Yorkshire farming family, was in mid-career and had already served for over 20 years as vicar of All Saints, South Wimbledon in a fast-expanding working-class parish. He was clearly an inspirational priest along with his wife and five children. He had moved to St Paul's, Lorrimore Square in 1902 before moving to St Mary Magdalene, Woolwich in 1908, shortly after Milner's ordination. He was joined by Milner six months later. They clearly respected one another, and Pickering was to spend the rest of his ministry in Woolwich until his death in 1933. Milner remained at St Mary Magdalene, Woolwich until later returning to King's as chaplain and college lecturer in history in July 1912, where he continued until the outbreak of war in August 1914.

There is again not a great deal of surviving material relating to Milner's four years in south London, but there is enough to piece together a picture from parish magazines, the local press and Milner's sermons, the latter of which survive in manuscript in Cambridge and York.[3]

St Paul's, Lorrimore Square is the church which Milner recorded later as having five Cambridge-educated clergy, all of whom had secured first-class honours degrees. Its neighbour, St Saviour's, the newly designated

---

[2]   Earlier Cambridge ordinands at St Paul's, Lorrimore Square include Arthur Duncan-Jones, see S. C. Carpenter, *Duncan-Jones of Chichester* (London: A. R. Mowbray's, 1956). Duncan-Jones was later one of the early college chaplains from 1905, seeking a Cambridge non-collegiate Anglican centre, initially St Anselm's, later the Oratory of the Good Shepherd.

[3]   Milner-White sermons, 1908–14, in manuscript, York Minster Archives, Milner-White Ms/EMW/XIX/1–24, also at King's College, KCAC/GBR/0272/EMW/2/15–16.

cathedral, also had a strong Cambridge presence in the figure of the sub-warden of its college, E. A. Edghill, an older contemporary of Milner's at King's.[4]

In both parishes, there was a team of clergy living near the church and the local Anglican school. On arrival at St Mary's, Milner became chaplain precentor, responsible for its services, liturgy and music, a suitable apprenticeship for his life-long ministry. His cricketing talents were quickly mobilized for the church choir team's match at Chislehurst, a few months later in 1909. The boy altar servers had a day's visit to Cambridge, taking in evensong at King's and tea at Clare. He similarly led a parish retreat to Cuddesdon, also taking responsibility for boys' work in the parish, including the Church Lads' Brigade as well as the "Quiet Sunday Evenings".[5]

As it happened, shortly after taking responsibility for the Church Lads' Brigade, it closed in December 1909, with the success of the Boy Scouts in the area seen as the cause. This seems to have caused a parish rethink and the setting up of a church-based Scout troop, which by 1912 had 40 members and an annual camping programme. Milner did not run the Scouts, but he was much influenced by this new and different way of doing "boys' work". Later, when he was dean, the King's College Choir School held annual camps from 1923 until 1939 at Batcombe in Somerset, run by Milner very much on Scout lines with a distinctive Anglican twist.[6] Similarly, Milner's only novel, written with Eleanor Duckett in 1938, *The Story of Hugh and Nancy*, and not great literature, has as its key motif the Scout and Girl Scout movements on both sides of the Atlantic.[7] Finally, in the late 1940s, the Scouts of the city of York

---

4   For Ernest Arthur Edghill (1879–1912), *Crockford's Clerical Directory*, 43rd edn, 1911, p. 452, which gives a very official picture of Edghill's frenetic energy in terms of scholarly, priestly, and social mission.

5   Church activities Parish Magazine St Mary Magdalene, Woolwich 1909–12, London Metropolitan Archive, P97/MRY/198–9.

6   Mary Holtby's memories of the Batcombe camps; see Holtby (ed.), *Milner-White: A Memorial*, p. 43.

7   Eric Milner-White and Eleanor Duckett, *The Story of Hugh and Nancy* (New York: Macmillan, 1938). Available in the Minster Library, York.

were allowed to hold their annual St George's Day special service of re-affirmation of the Scout promise and law in the Minster, and then to parade through the city, as they still do.[8]

It is likely that it was the Revd Ernest Arthur Edghill (1879–1912), the sub-warden at St Saviour's College, Southwark, who had the greatest influence on the young priest in Woolwich. As noted earlier, Edghill may have been a Trappist. Educated at Eton, he had been an older undergraduate contemporary of Milner at King's, studying in 1903 for a BD at King's College, London. Now almost entirely forgotten, owing to his early death in 1912, he was a scholarly phenomenon at King's as an undergraduate, with a double first in classics and theology (1901–2). He was the son of the Revd John Cox Edghill (1835–1917), an Anglo-Catholic who had done parish work at St Mark's, Whitechapel before becoming an army chaplain, subsequently rising to be Chaplain-General to the Forces from 1885 until 1901.[9]

Arthur Edghill had been ordained deacon in 1904. The same year, he won the Cambridge Hulsean Prize, and four years later the Norrisian, both in theology, the latter being a foretaste of a fuller study of the protestant German philosopher Albrecht Ritschl, published in 1910. He had been a tutor at the Kelham Hall, the theological college run by the Society of the Sacred Mission, between 1907 and 1908 before joining the clerical team at Southwark Cathedral as vice-principal of St Saviour's College at the same time as Milner moved to the nearby St Paul's, Lorrimore Square. His academic reputation led him to give the Hulsean Lectures in Cambridge in 1910 at the age of 31, having also become a lecturer in church history at King's College, London in 1907.[10]

---

[8]   For St Saviour's College work with boys, see its magazine, *London Bridge*, 1910–13, largely written and created by Edghill and with material by Milner, including his account of the Passion Play at Oberammergau in 1910, and writings of Edghill on the relationship between faith and his Scouting work. KCAC/Modern Archives/GBR/0272 /EMW 4/2/1.

[9]   John Cox Edghill, deacon and priest St Mark's, Whitechapel, 1858–62, army chaplain 1862–85, Chaplain-General to the Forces 1885–1901.

[10] For Ritschl, *ODCC*, p. 1400; E. A. Edghill, *Fact and Faith: A Study of Ritschlianism* (London: Macmillan, 1910).

A man of ascetic temperament, he clearly made a deep impression on Milner through his frenetic energy in Southwark, as evidenced by the St Saviour's College magazine, copies of which remained with Milner throughout his life. Along with his theological interests and lecturing in second-century Christian history, he was passionately committed to "boys'" work, especially that of the Boy Scouts, and a troop was formed at St Saviour's. It was at their Scout camp in 1912, just after Milner had left to return to Cambridge, that Edghill was accidentally killed by a self-inflicted wound from an axe. Milner conducted the memorial service in Woolwich, giving the eulogy on 30 August 1912, published later by the *Church Times*.[11]

As well as influencing Milner in the direction of "boys' work", itself part of Milner's earlier visionary experience, Edghill was one of Milner's close friends contributing to the formation of his priestly character, along with Will Spens, Philip Loyd and Oscar Browning. Milner never presented himself as either a theologian or a philosopher, upon which Michael Ramsey later expressed some regret.[12] Nor was Milner that interested in academic theology, history, or art history, as will become clear. But he was influenced by Edghill's critique of Ritschl, and what Edghill saw as the formlessness of contemporary idealist German theology, which Milner expressed in his earliest known publication in August 1914. This took the form of a rather callow review of the American Quaker academic theologian Rufus M. James' book *Spiritual Reformers of the Sixteenth and Seventeenth Centuries*, in which Milner concludes that Quaker theology, like that of Ritschl, was "pure religion undefiled by religious experience". In Milner's opinion, "the Reformation was a Revolt that sought that".[13]

One of the main original sources for Milner in the years in south London and Cambridge before 1914 and later are the manuscripts of his sermons, of which he gave many, usually at least weekly. Wilkinson states that Milner was not good at delivering sermons, talking above

---

[11]   *Church Times*, 23, 30 August 1912, pp. 210–11, 238–9.
[12]   Ramsey in Pare and Harris, *Milner-White: A Memoir*, p. 101.
[13]   Eric Milner-White, "Mystics of the Reformation", review of Rufus M. James, *Spiritual Reformers of the Sixteenth and Seventeenth Centuries*, in *Comment and Criticism: A Cambridge Quarterly* 2:2 (August 1914), pp. 98–104.

the heads of his congregation, addressing as it were a "higher" audience in tones and language which were ecstatic, almost mystical.[14] On first reading today, one can see his point, and yet throughout the interwar period Milner was invited from early in 1918 to preach in prominent London churches, including St Paul's Cathedral, Westminster Abbey and All Saints, Margaret Street, as well as at the anniversary in 1933 in Oxford of John Keble's famous assize sermon of 1833. While Wilkinson and others may be right, and we do not have any copies of doubtless extempore sermons delivered to soldiers on the Western Front, the modern reader must be missing something. Much of the same reaction is produced on reading some of his prayers. In general, however, when given a specific brief, his prayers are more disciplined and effective, as his collection *After the Third Collect* shows, and most notably in the wonderful bidding prayer of Christmas Eve 1918, just six weeks after the Armistice—probably his most enduring legacy in a long life.

What is today's reader missing? This writer is no literary or liturgical scholar, so what follows must simply be a suggestion, that what is lacking is an understanding of the Anglo-Catholic mood of the period from 1910 until the 1930s, something which Adrian Hastings recognized, but few religious/church historians have prioritized.[15] In the English reformed tradition, the sermon took on a specifically exhortatory and explicatory role in public worship, through the priority given to Matins in the Book of Common Prayer and a sermon based on the lessons of the day, often delivered from the prominently positioned pulpit. For Anglo-Catholics, the sermon is more closely tied to the act of worship itself, and the greater significance given to the Eucharist with the receiving of the bread and the wine—the sacraments. Milner was not alone in preaching in this fashion of exaltation. Father Waggett, for instance, a Cowley Father, prominent in both the ancient universities before 1914, also later a chaplain in the trenches and an important influence on Milner in 1918,

---

[14]   Wilkinson, *Milner-White*, p. 28.

[15]   Adrian Hastings, *A History of English Christianity 1920–1985* (London: Collins, 1986).

and on the Oratory of the Good Shepherd, preached in a similar style.[16] Other chaplains appointed to Cambridge colleges before 1914 shared many of the same principles and practices, which became an element in the distinctive Anglican tone in Cambridge at that time, referred to by Archbishop Ramsey in his own memoir of Milner in 1965.

Another factor may be relevant in Milner's case. The importance of the late seventeenth-century Anglican divines has already been noted in Milner's earlier spiritual development, most notably the writings of Thomas Traherne. It is not wholly unreasonable to see echoes of those writings in his later sermonizing.

These sermons deserve more scholarly analysis than is possible here, but for completeness here are just a few examples. On Trinity Sunday 1909, Milner focussed the worshipper's attention on the need to become "more God like" and seeing the power of Christ crucified. In the following years, among other themes, he concentrated on the role of the "will" in religion, and on the "humiliation of Christ sacrificed", which concluded that "Sacrifice is the very nature of God". In 1912, he preached about the difficulty of talking about "worship" and that is "because we dare not say it, because worship is above unselfishness, above prayer, above love even, for it is the perfection of love". These sermons were like verbal incense, spiritual but not readily comprehensible.[17] Whether they were delivered in the tones later characterized by many as "precious", we do not know, but the words, enunciation, ritual and music of Anglo-Catholic worship of the time were later wickedly parodied by Alan Bennett in *Beyond the Fringe* in 1960.

---

[16]   Philip Napier Waggett (1862–1939): *ODNB*, vol. 56, p. 691. Also J. Nias, *Flame from an Oxford Cloister: The Life and Writings of Philip Napier Waggett* (London: Faith Press, 1961). Cowley Fathers: the colloquial name for the Society of St John the Evangelist in Cowley, Oxford.

[17]   For good examples of this style of preaching before 1914, see YML, Milner-White Ms/EMW/XI/1–24. For his later style of preaching, see Milner's address to the Southampton Anglo-Catholic Congress in 1925, *Church Times*, 26 June 1925, p. 762, or "The Incarnation and the Church", in Humphrey Beevor (ed.), *Catholic Sermons* (London: SPCK, 1932), pp. 89–93, publ. for the English Church Union.

As has been mentioned in the preface, Milner destroyed almost all his personal papers. The only surviving exceptions are Milner's letters to Oscar Browning and his small collection of letters to Arthur Wayment, headteacher, neighbour and church warden at St Mary Magdalene in Woolwich.

As with his letters to Browning, the Wayment letters are significant.

First, Wayment's son, Hilary, became Milner's first godson in 1912.[18] Milner's response to the invitation was ecstatic, with an almost obsessive correspondence about the boy's potential baptismal name, providing early hints of the trait of "perfectionism" in Milner's character. Given this preliminary, Hilary may have found his godfather's interest oppressive at times. It was certainly influential and, after education at Charterhouse and King's, and a professional career including the British Council, he became the most significant scholar of the stained glass in King's College Chapel in the decades following Milner's death.[19]

Secondly, the Wayment collection also contains the only known surviving letters from Milner at the Western Front from 1914 until 1917/18, including the month of June 1915 during the battle of Festubert, a terrible foreshadowing of the battle of the Somme a year later.

In reading any of these writings, it is important to remember that Milner was not a theologian/philosopher, or well versed in the history of the Ancient World and its literature. He was a historian, educated by teachers at Harrow and King's who had been nurtured within late Victorian conventions, for whom the transformations within the historical discipline coming from Ranke and his disciples were only slowly percolating down to undergraduate teaching.[20] He was also a young man whose moderately conservative family values had been reinforced by his undergraduate studies and reading. All his early experience had been very Anglo-centric, affirming his belief in the strength of nation and nationality in human history.

---

18   KCAC/Modern Archives/GBR/0272/EMW/X/2/Wayment/1–2.

19   Hilary Wayment (1912–2005): Wikipedia.

20   Leopold von Ranke (1795–1886): Late nineteenth-century German historian and pioneer of modern empirical historicism, with its focus on documentary evidence, in particular.

5

Return to King's, 1912–14

In the summer of 1912, Milner returned to King's as chaplain to Dean Brooke, and any account of these years relies on his letters to the now-retired Browning. They give the impression of personal happiness at reconnecting with undergraduates and no hint of the personal shyness, later expressed by Wilkinson.[1] There is also a light-heartedness of the young don, recorded many years later by Seiriol Evans, an undergraduate at King's at the time, later Dean of Gloucester, and chairman of the Central Council for the Care of Churches, of which Milner was also a member. He records an overnight "jape" led by the chaplain, probably in Trinity term 1914, on the river to Ely to view the cathedral at dawn, after frying sausages—Boy Scout-like—overnight on the bank. Finding access locked, nothing daunted and following a long tradition of climbing into college, the chaplain effected an entry, doubtless followed by others.[2] Milner during these years was not yet certain of his priestly direction between continuing in Cambridge or joining an Anglican monastic order such as the Community of the Resurrection at Mirfield in West Yorkshire.[3] The only irritant reported to Browning was the attitude of the Fellows towards the chapel, in particular their resistance to a memorial tablet to Arthur Edghill, with Milner writing:

> I have quite failed to stir up any desire for a memorial tablet
> to Edghill in King's—indeed one is so coldly met at the mere

---

[1]   Milner to Browning, 1912–14, KCAC, Modern MS, GBR/0272/OB.

[2]   Pare and Harris, *Milner-White: A Memoir*, pp. 1–2.

[3]   Milner, uncertain of career direction 1912–14, in letter to Wayment, April 1914, KCAC, EMW/X/2/Wayment.

mention that it is most unpleasant to try at all ... Few men can
have made disciples so enthusiastic, almost at a touch. But this
is not understood, indeed is incredible at King's. The walls of
the chapel are meant, I guess, to celebrate classical scholars, not
Christian apostles.[4]

But along with this personal contentment a lot had changed among the
community of college chaplains and deans during Milner's absence from
Cambridge since 1907. It was into this changed atmosphere that Milner
threw himself over the next couple of years.[5]

As earlier noted, much of the popular writing about the university of
Cambridge before 1914 is dominated by the Apostles, with their sceptical
agnosticism. But there was also intellectual vigour within scholarly
Anglicanism in this period, despite the earlier public disputations on
ritualism and the debates on the relationship of science and theology.[6]

But despite this renewed energy, there was less interest more generally
in Christian theology outside the English-speaking world, especially that
in the French and German tradition, both Catholic and Reformed. It
is not very clear why this should have been, other than it relied on the
ability to read the literature in French and German. Possibly also relevant
is that Anglican/Roman Catholic relations were inevitably affected by the
much broader Irish dimension within British life, both nationally and
internationally, including those with the Vatican. In this area, and despite
the robust declaration of papal infallibility and the Vatican Decrees
(1869–70), the pontificate of Leo XIII (1878–1903) seemed relatively
liberal until the very elderly pontiff, rather uncharacteristically, forcibly
declared Anglican priestly orders invalid in his encyclical *Apostolicae
curae* (1896).

---

[4]   Milner-White to Browning, 12 November 1912, KCAC/0272/OB/1/1112/A.

[5]   Pare and Harris, *Milner-White: A Memoir*, pp. 93–6.

[6]   For Modernism: *ODCC*, p. 1098. For leading Modernists: Alfred F. Loisy
      (1857–1940), *ODCC*, p. 993; George Tyrell (1861–1909), *ODCC*, p. 1649;
      Baron F. von Hügel (1852–1925), *ODCC*, p. 1707. See also Bernard Reardon,
      Roman Catholic Modernism (Stanford: University Press, 1970), pp. 9–65.

His successor on the other hand, Pope Pius X (1903–14), opened a generalized onslaught on theological "Modernism" in his papal decree *Lamentabili sane exitu* and his later encyclical *Pascendi dominici gregis* (both 1907).

Not surprisingly, these moves agitated younger, academic Anglo-Catholic clergy particularly, along with some of their British Roman Catholic peers and reformist Roman Catholics in northern Europe and North America. For our purposes, the cause célèbre centred on the figure of Father Tyrell (1861–1909), an Anglo-Irish Jesuit priest who became the object of papal discipline, leading to his expulsion from the Jesuit order (1906) and excommunication in 1908. This had implications in Cambridge, as the university had seen a growth in religious and theological interest from about 1905, as shown by the membership of the Christian Society, the activities of the Anglo-Catholic undergraduate society (STC—Confraternity of the Holy Trinity, founded in 1857) and the later success of the mission to the university in 1913, along with the arrival of a group of young Anglo-Catholic college chaplains during these years, of whom Milner was the newest member in 1912. Milner was not directly involved in the theological debates about Roman Catholic Modernism. Nevertheless, he was clearly part of the cultural atmosphere among college chaplains responding to the challenges posed by the Vatican reactions to the writings of Loisy and Tyrell. For them, the emphasis was on the historical evolution of catholic truths, sacramental worship and spiritual understanding, all elements within Milner's ongoing priestly development.

Collectively, they were reformist in religious practice within their own chapels, often interested in theological Modernism and conscious that Anglican resources in Cambridge, outside the colleges, were less than those available in Oxford. From about 1906, a group of chaplains and some others set about finding a residential base and mission akin to a combination of Pusey House and the Cowley Fathers in Oxford, to be called St Anselm's. Inspired by H. L. Pass, a layman, and Father Waggett, they were able to acquire a house and appoint a warden, Father Wilfred

Knox, and some residents.[7] Progress was slow in articulating what sort of association it should be. There were differences of personality and views and not much clarity had been achieved by 1912. Milner's return to Cambridge in the autumn of that year energized the group, as recorded by Dean Carpenter of Exeter many years later, and provided a "vision" for what such a development should be. Progress was stalled with the outbreak of war in August 1914. Even so, interest was already being expressed by some Anglican priests in East Africa by the middle of the war. However, what became the Oratory of the Good Shepherd was not formally instituted until 1919, with the opening of Oratory House in 1920. At that time, an agreed Rule was still evolving, with Milner a critical and central figure.[8] This was to be influenced by, but not copied from, the Oratorian order in the Roman Catholic Church, with its celibate priestly Anglican members being inspired by the seventeenth-century settlement of Little Gidding, founded in 1626 by Nicholas Farrer and his family in Huntingdonshire, the object of Milner's historical research as chaplain.

---

[7]   S. C. Carpenter (Dean of Exeter), letter to the *Church Times*, 30 June 1950, p. 490, writing about the interest among Cambridge Anglo-Catholics in the writings of Father Tyrell at this time through Leonard Pass, including Will Spens, Gordon Selwyn, Geoffrey Clayton, John How, Arthur Duncan-Jones and himself, enhanced later by Father Waggett at Great St Mary's. George Tibbatts, *Oratory*, pp. 1–6; *John How, Parish Priest, Cambridge Don, Scottish Primus: A Biography* (Oxford: Becket, 1983). John How was president of the STC from 1910–24.

[8]   Tibbatts, *Oratory*, pp. 8–9, including Milner's "Ideal for the Oratory"; also Pare and Harris, *Milner-White: A Memoir*, pp. 94–6 for the text of the Seven Rules, again written by Milner in 1918.

6

First World War, 1914–18

In the years before August 1914, Milner had expressed no anxieties about the rivalries of the great powers. He was not untypical, having already largely lost engagement with domestic politics and international affairs, despite his years in Southwark. But as with so many young Oxbridge graduates, he volunteered almost immediately following the outbreak of war. He was interviewed by Bishop Taylor-Smith, Chaplain-General to the Forces, whose notes survive. Taylor-Smith clearly knew Milner as a high churchman from his comments relating to his curacies in south London and may have known more in that Arthur Edghill's father had been Taylor-Smith's predecessor as Chaplain-General. Despite Taylor-Smith's reputation as an evangelical, his decision was a definitive "YES".[1] Milner formally became a temporary chaplain to the Forces in December 1914, serving on the Western Front in the 7th Division almost continuously until early 1918, having been promoted to senior chaplain in early 1917.

Once again, we are left with only fragments of personal evidence, and official War Office papers relating to Milner's service as a temporary chaplain (4th class) are quite formal. His service was largely linked to the Welsh Fusiliers, the South Staffordshire, the Queen's West Surrey, and the Warwickshire regiments, certainly until his promotion in early 1917.

As with the earlier urban settlement movement before 1914, the tone of the historiography about the contribution of army chaplains

---

[1]   Taylor-Smith's acceptance. Howson at Milner seminar 2016 at the University of York.

during the First World War has changed considerably since the 1960s.[2] In Milner's case, there are only a few surviving letters to the Wayment family, and a typed copy of a diary letter to his parents in the second phase of the battle of Festubert in the first half of June 1915.[3] Thereafter, there is nothing beyond some correspondence, whilst on leave, with M. R. James (Provost of King's) later in 1915. Nevertheless, they support the revisionist perspective.

The earlier material shows how assumptions about the role of army chaplains had to change rapidly as the shape of the conflict evolved. At first, Milner is working as chaplain and hospital orderly fully behind the lines at the main field hospital, describing himself as having officer-type responsibilities in two hospitals with 600 casualties in association with the Royal Army Medical Corps. But the solidifying of the military terrain soon created an interconnected system of frontline trenches, reserve trenches, and first aid and injury stations, with stretcher rescuers including the non-combatant chaplains moving up and down the lines. Simultaneously, they were carrying out their more obviously priestly functions to the already dead or dying in the frontline. Milner's diary letter was composed after his troops had been at the frontline in the second half of May and had been relieved on 31 May. Milner was therefore immediately behind the frontline before the troops returned there in mid-June, at which point he takes his first period of home leave since arriving in France the previous October. Even this short fragment describing his days, conscious of the censor, shows his ability as a descriptive writer and reporter. But he had also written to the Provost, M. R. James, describing battle on 15 June 1915:

---

[2]   For recent writing on the Chaplaincy Service: Linda Parker, *The Whole Armour of God: Anglican Army Chaplains in the Great War* (Amherst, MA and Warwick: Helion, 2013); Michael Snape and Edward Madigan (eds), *The Clergy in Khaki: New Perspectives on British Army Chaplains in the First World War* (Farnham: Ashgate, 2013); Michael Snape, "Church of England Army Chaplains in the First World War: Goodbye to 'Good Bye to All That'", *Journal of Ecclesiastical History* 62:2 (April 2011), pp. 318–45.

[3]   Wayment letters from late 1914, Festubert diary, 1–21 June 1915, KCAC/ Modern Archives/GBR/EMW/X/1–2/Wayment.

(Battle) is indescribable, unimaginable. The fresh night air was itself a rushing road like a waterfall, as a thousand shells tore through it. The dark blue sky was lit up by a summer lightning flash upward from the earth every second. The darker motionless clumps of poplars all around the horizon were continuously silhouetted in white flame. The continuous firework of light balls went up from the German trenches. But most awesome was the noise. We felt so powerless against those splitting cracks and roars, and dreamt of the metal tearing its way into bodies of poor men.[4]

The impact of these early experiences prompted a group of Anglo-Catholic army chaplains to prepare a volume of essays on their own feelings, and publication under the editorship of F. B. MacNutt, who had been a canon of Southwark at the same time as Milner had been in Woolwich. The volume, *The Church in the Furnace*, was published in November 1917, with Milner contributing the chapter on "Worship and Services". Reviews were respectful, but no one could disguise the credentials of the writers, four of whom were awarded the DSO during the conflict, including Milner in mid-1917. They were brave men.

In this situation, Milner stresses how inappropriate the pattern of regular parish worship had been in the trenches, the routine of Sunday Matins and evensong with only an early celebration of Holy Communion, and how lacking in meaning and relevance were the set prayers and canticles of the Book of Common Prayer. Evening communions, especially before battle, the use of the reserved sacrament at the front itself for the injured and dying, the prayers and responses for the burial of the dead on the battlefield, all needed endorsement.[5] Similarly, the atmosphere of regular worship behind the frontline should be "more homely" and inclusive, with full use of the reformed tradition of hymn singing, which French Catholic priests envied. Among other elements was the question of how difficult it was for the worshipper, in both war

---

[4]   Nash, "A Right Prelude to Christmas", in Massing and Zeeman (eds), *King's College Chapel 1515–2015*, pp. 323–43.

[5]   Reserved Sacrament, see informative entry on Wikipedia.

and peace, to understand and absorb the value of personal prayer as well as its part in collective worship. Milner used the concept of "the Loneliness of Prayer" as a way of thinking. These experiences and insights needed to be carried over into peacetime through reform of the 1662 Prayer Book for colleges and parishes alike.[6]

This 1917 essay has been discussed in some detail as it remained in one form or another Milner's best general statement on worship, prayer, and liturgy on the occasions that marked each new beginning in his ministry—on his election as Dean of King's in April 1918, on the first meeting of the full Chapter of York Minster in the spring of 1942, and in his elegiac farewell to the Church Union in 1962.

The book's publication in November 1917 followed a personal crisis for Milner in July which was expressed in letters to Arthur Wayment:

> Much of my work has been burying hundreds of British who have been out since July and November 1916. I leave the horror of it to your imagination (EMW to Wayment, 16 April 1917).

> I am mentally and spiritually exhausted, now that my three years of war is coming to end (EMW to Wayment, 24 June 1917).

He felt torn between loyalty to his present task (his existing short-term contract ended in April 1918) and anxiety about what to do on return to the UK, as between remaining as chaplain or joining an Anglican religious community. In the end, he saw out his contract, moving to the Italian front early in 1918:

> I am staying on here for another year of this horror out here, not feeling it right to come back (EMW to Wayment, 25 October 1917)[7]

---

[6]   Eric Milner-White, "Worship and Services", in F. B. MacNutt (ed.), *The Church in the Furnace: Essays by Seventeen Temporary Church of England Chaplains on Active Service in France and Flanders* (London: Macmillan, 1917), pp. 175–212.

[7]   Milner-White to Wayment, 16 April 1917, 24 June 1917, 25 October 1917 and no date, KCAC/EMW/2/Wayment/1–2.

But before that point, he committed two conspicuous acts of bravery, for one of which he was awarded the DSO in the 1918 New Year's Honours. The first was the reburial of fellow chaplain the Hon. Maurice Peel, a well-known figure as the son of Viscount Peel, former Speaker of the House of Commons, and grandson of the Prime Minister, Sir Robert Peel. He was also in the 7th Division. Already a widower, ten years older than Milner, and a close friend, he had enlisted as a chaplain in 1914, becoming well known for his intrepid courage in "going over the top" unarmed along with his men. Also attached to the Welsh Fusiliers and so part of the team including Milner at the battle of Festubert in May and June 1915, he had been injured and returned home, but later returned to the front, to be killed almost immediately by a sniper in trying to rescue an injured soldier on 14 May 1917 in the second battle of Bullecourt. Buried by his men in an unmarked grave, he had recently been awarded a Bar to his earlier Military Cross. On 17 May (Ascension Day), Milner, recently promoted to senior chaplain, returned to the site with two soldiers in daylight and gave Peel a Christian burial, reading the Collect for the day (Peel's favourite).[8]

The second was the action for which he was awarded the DSO. The description of the action itself only exists in an account in the 1965 memoir by Pare and Harris, but the formal recommendation for the award higher up the command chain is in the National Archives. There must be some doubt as to the details, but the account in Pare and Harris is plausible. The Pare family were well-known friends of Milner in Canterbury; Pare had been at King's, ordained in 1935, and in 1963 was Provost of Wakefield, and joint editor of the memoir of 1965. In addition, his unmarried sister, Erica, had joined Eric in York as his housekeeper/assistant. The 1965 account may owe much to her and her brother's memories of private conversations. According to this account, a platoon in battle at the frontline had lost both of its young officers. In this circumstance, not uncommon, the standing orders were that the corporal should take command. But in this case, the soldiers asked Milner if he, as a "non-combatant", would take over. He did so successfully. As a result,

---

[8]   Entry on Peel in Winchester College online publication, Winchester College at War.com (2024).

he was recommended (not for the first time) for a bravery award, as it turned out the DSO, second only to the Victoria Cross.

The story in Pare and Harris then gets less clear, recording that Chaplain-General Taylor-Smith deeply disliked this breaking of regulations and "cashiered" him, sending him back to the UK. This is certainly not true; Milner remained with his regiments until April 1918 but had moved to the Italian front in late 1917. What may be true is that Milner's actions, as a recently promoted chaplain, may have disturbed Taylor-Smith in that, twice in a short period, one of his senior chaplaincy staff had certainly acted bravely, but also foolishly through endangering the lives not only of himself but also the soldiers who accompanied him in daylight to perform a Christian burial in the case of Maurice Peel. The Pare and Harris account may have been an embellishment or a conflation of the two separate acts.

The announcement was made in the New Year's Honours in 1918, and Milner remained in the chaplaincy service until April, when he chose not to be re-engaged. Pressure to return to Cambridge was also coming from the university itself. John How pressed that Milner should be released to pick up the pieces in relation to the Oratory of the Good Shepherd. Father Waggett (himself strongly linked with the OGS pre-war, and in 1918 a chaplain in the forces, also in the 7th Division) strongly urged Milner personally that he should not seek admission to Mirfield, but that his post-war ministry should be in Cambridge and the wider Anglo-Catholic community. But events intervened; the Fellows of King's made that decision by electing Milner as dean in succession to Brooke in April 1918. Milner accepted.[9]

Summation: Milner in 1918

Milner's interpretation of the English catholic tradition was pretty fully developed in outline and practice by 1918, remaining remarkably unchanged over the following 45 years in two very different "cathedral-like" situations—one collegiate, the other provincial.

---

[9]   On Father Waggett, see Wilkinson, *Milner-White*, p. 12.

But in what did that constancy consist, and how was it grounded in what might be called the Anglican way of thinking?

Returning to King's as chaplain in 1912 had drawn him into a religious, theological, and philosophical environment that called upon his temperamental disposition to get involved directly, not simply academically. As an undergraduate he had been a very successful historian with a particular interest in English ecclesiastical history, especially that of the seventeenth century, and the writings of the Caroline divines in poetry, prose, and prayer. He had done some research on the community established by Nicholas Ferrar at Little Gidding in the 1630s.

As one of the chaplains on the Western Front, he had fashioned a critique of pre-war conventional Anglican parochial practice—something which he had not done before 1914 despite his experience in Southwark. His essay in *The Church in the Furnace* contained elements that were to inform his practical churchmanship throughout his long career.

In 1918, he was about to make his distinctive contribution over the next 20 years as a very individual Dean of King's, a prolific writer of prayers, and as a choreographer of Anglican worship. He was also a vigorous participant and public controversialist in debates around the distinctive integrity of the catholic ecclesiology of the Church of England. In all these areas of engagement, his perspective was historical and increasingly aesthetic, reflecting as it inevitably did some of the earlier contemporary crosscurrents within the historical discipline in the decade before 1914. To this was added his own growing preoccupation with the concept of "beauty" as a benchmark for many aspects of human life. In the many hair-splitting attempts to define Anglo-Catholicism, the category of modernizing, moderate Prayer Book Catholic probably gets closest, as it does for his distinguished pupil and friend, Archbishop Michael Ramsey.

Unsurprisingly therefore, Milner approached ecclesiology and Anglican identity as a priestly church historian. Almost of necessity, his focus was on England and was conservative philosophically. Milner did not leave a corpus of writing on the subject. However, he did publish a short book in 1939, entitled *Anglican Piety*, which in less than 30 pages gives his outline history of English catholicism, both before and after the Reformation, and through which he traces the evolving identity of the Church in England. It is short, crisp, and clear, always Milner's best mode in composing prayers and critical pieces.[10]

Milner in pre-1914 Cambridge had been among the final generation of undergraduates and ordinands whose frame of mind was formed in the philosophical atmosphere of late nineteenth-century English idealism, which had become so pervasive after 1880. As we have seen in his votes in the debates at Oscar Browning's Political Society at King's from 1904 to 1907, Milner's emphasis was on "nationality" as the driving force of historical change, and that the Reformation, while politically dramatic, had not fundamentally changed the English "character". As an approach, it focussed more on the narrative than the scientific, being more organic and dialectical. Such a methodology was likely to be particularly attractive to any historian from a high church family. His booklet of 1939 charts the chronology of English Catholicism, beginning with the Scriptures and the early councils and creeds (properly understood historically), and progressing swiftly through the Gregorian reforms in the eleventh century towards the changes in the late Middle Ages with the simultaneous evolution of national Christian traditions (Gallicanism) and the increasing ambitions of the papacy (Ultramontanism). This was the broader context within which Henry VIII decided to split from papal authority in 1534. Flowing from that essentially political action, Milner saw the forging of a more distinctive English catholic ecclesiology over the next century until the restoration of the monarchy in 1660. During this period, the Book of Common Prayer, and the King James Bible (critically

---

[10]   Eric Milner-White, *Anglican Piety* (London: SPCK Little Books of Religion, No. 157, 1939). For a much earlier version, see Milner's address to the Catholic Literature Association in May 1921 in which many of the elements of *Anglican Piety* are discussed, especially his views on the Council of Trent, and the idea that faith before printing was conveyed largely through art in churches and cathedrals: *Church Times*, 13 May 1921, p. 455. At the same period, Milner gave a series of lectures at Church House, Westminster on Anglo-Catholicism under the later Stuarts, which brought applause at the mention of Charles I and Laud, with Milner emphasizing that restraint and dignity were the prominent features of the later Caroline Church: *Church Times*, 21 October 1921, p. 377.

in English) had become canonical texts, informed by an Anglican catholic ecclesiology of the via media, articulated most influentially by the cleric Richard Hooker.[11]

In this critical text for Anglican high churchmen such as Milner, Christian doctrinal "authority" was seen as standing on three foundations. For them, Christian doctrine in England had evolved in a "morphological" manner, involving three streams—the Scriptures and the writings of the Fathers of the Church, the historical teachings of the Church, and (critically) the exercise of individual informed reason.

Fundamental for Milner himself were the writings of Lancelot Andrewes, especially his *Preces Privatae*, the ecclesiology of Archbishop Laud, and the style of late seventeenth-century Anglican worship in respect of doctrine, liturgy, and practice. This should be dignified, restrained, and fitting for the occasion and place. Alongside this was Milner's high regard for seventeenth-century Anglican poetry, literature, and hymns, including Donne, Milton, Traherne, Bishop Ken and Isaac Watts. The long-lasting impact of his required reading programme for the Lightfoot Scholarship in 1904, with a set thesis topic on the controversial Puritan cleric Richard Baxter, had been substantial.

Within this historic evolution, Milner was always appreciative of the Oxford Movement's early intentions in trying to rectify the lack of church discipline, doctrinal sloppiness, and subservience to an increasingly Whiggish reformism of many political and church leaders of the age. He also approved of some of the developments in the Church of England that flowed from the Oxford reformers, with its greater emphasis on the writers of the early Church, the centrality of the sacraments, the revival of Anglican religious monasticism, and a more spiritual and scholarly training for ordinands in association with Christian education more generally. But there was a reservation in that some of the Oxford Movement's most prominent figures had converted to Rome from the late 1840s, with Newman, Manning, Robert Wilberforce, Faber, and others setting new possible directions for Anglican high churchmen to follow.

---

[11]   Richard Hooker, *Of the laws of Ecclesiastical polity* (Cambridge: Texts in the History of Political Thought, 2008); Anthony Quinton, *The Politics of Imperfection* (London: Faber & Faber, 1978), pp. 9–28.

It is noticeable that Milner is never more than respectful of Newman. Much more esteemed in Milner's eyes were John Keble and E. B. Pusey, and the later churchmen and writers associated with the publication of *Lux Mundi* in 1889.[12]

This is comprehensible given that Milner's life coincided with the unexpected developments within the Roman Catholic Church after 1870, particularly the pontificate of Pius X (1903–14), precisely the decade of Milner's own priestly development at Cambridge and Southwark. The papal onslaught on Modernism in 1908 and later the pursuit of the Anglo-Irish Jesuit priest Father Tyrell had a particular impact on the group of Cambridge theological and liturgical modernists with whom Milner was associated. More broadly, the earlier declaration by Leo XIII (1878–1903) of the invalidity of Anglican priestly orders struck at the centre of Anglican ecclesiological doctrine of one catholic, apostolic, and universal church of the creeds, reaffirmed each week by the congregation of the faithful.[13]

As an interpretation of the history of the catholic tradition, *Anglican Piety* was devoted to the developments in the catholic version of the faith over the centuries, particularly from the late fifteenth century across Europe until the Council of Trent (1545–63). Its view of the sixteenth-century European Reformers was narrowly English, its attitude to the impact of Puritanism, seventeenth-century nonconformity, and Methodism was largely ignored. Its perspective on the seventeenth-century European scientific revolution and the later Enlightenment was passed over. It was a very monocular view, even at the time.

---

[12]   *Lux Mundi* (1889), edited by Charles Gore, a volume of significant published essays in the development of Anglican catholic understanding.

[13]   Catholic (lower-case catholic), as in the creeds, usually read as an adjective. See *ODCC*, pp. 305–6.

7

Cambridge, 1918–41: A very individual dean

An individual modernizer

While Milner's Anglo-Catholic churchmanship was stable by 1918, his personal qualities and traits became more pronounced during the interwar years within a mix that made up a complex man.

The first was that, although a figure of character and foibles as dean well known among the Fellows and undergraduates generally, he is also described widely as "shy" among the college community. This was particularly so outside the circle of those closely involved with chapel worship and potential ordination.[1] This was not a feature noted before 1914, indeed rather the reverse. The spree to Ely described by Seiriol Evans' anecdote earlier, and his years as an army chaplain with his evident success with the troops, seem at odds with a later shyness.

Second, his concern with faith, worship, and churchmanship to the exclusion of almost all national and global affairs since his decision on ordination in 1905 is perplexing. In 1918, with a moderately high-profile Church position, closely intertwined with the ancient universities and the state, it seems positively bizarre. This impression is reinforced by the fact that many leading Anglican churchmen, led by William Temple and others, were actively committed to a more socially and politically engaged Church at home, and with the promotion of international peace and order across the world. Nor would Milner have lacked daily conversation on these matters among his colleagues at King's, who

---

[1] On Milner's shyness, see Wilkinson, *Milner-White*, p. 18.

included John Maynard Keynes, G. Lowes Dickinson, A. C. Pigou, and J. H. Clapham—all men of diverse experience of the world at large. It is, however, almost impossible to find Milner writing, preaching, or being reported as saying anything on social and international affairs in the interwar period or later.

Third, the aspect again visible before 1914 but not prominent, was his increasingly artistic interests and a growing aestheticism, all of which were given much fuller expression in the 1930s and after his move to York, coinciding with his growing personal wealth through inheritance and canny financial investment.

It would be easy to speculate about these tendencies, linking them to his experiences during the Great War, but we do not have the evidence.

The new dean

Nine Lessons and Carols

Elected as the incoming dean in April 1918, and before the Armistice, it was immediately clear that this was to be a new phase, the first evidence of which can be seen in Milner's address to the governing body immediately following his election. In this, he had moulded his general critique of pre-war parish worship in *The Church in the Furnace* into a vision of the national role that the great Anglican churches, chapels, and cathedrals might play in the religious life of the nation. Later, six weeks after the Armistice on 11 November, he was to show this intent with King's College Chapel holding its first Service of Nine Lessons and Carols on Christmas Eve, outside term, and so for "town and gown" alike. Inspired by a service prepared for Truro Cathedral by Bishop Benson in 1880, different versions of a Christmas Eve service had been promoted locally over the succeeding years, but without any "special" authority. But in the case of 1918 at King's, it touched a different chord, locally, nationally, and, gradually, throughout the English-speaking Christian world. At this first King's service, the elements highlighted in Milner's address to the governing council a few months earlier were brought together—an inspiring musical liturgy along with additional readings and special prayers in a service supplementary to, but consistent with, the Book of Common Prayer.

What is in no doubt is that the opening bidding prayer, written by Milner himself, became a key element, progressively used all over the English-speaking world. It is worth reminding ourselves of its words and the very specific context in which Milner wrote them:

> Beloved in Christ, be it this Christmastide our joy and our delight to hear again the message of the angels, and in heart and mind to go even unto Bethlehem and see this thing that has come to pass, and the Babe lying in a manger.
>
> Therefore, let us read and mark in Holy Scripture the tale of the loving purposes of God from the first days of our disobedience unto the glorious Redemption brought us by this Holy Child.
>
> But first, let us pray for the needs of the whole world; for peace on earth and goodwill among all his people; for unity and brotherhood within the Church he came to build.
>
> And because this of all things would rejoice his heart, let us remember, in his name, the poor and helpless, the cold, the hungry, and the oppressed; the sick and them that mourn, the lonely and the unloved, the aged and the little children; all those who know not the Lord Jesus, or who love him not, or who by sin have grieved his heart of love.
>
> Lastly, let us remember before God all those who rejoice with us, but upon another shore, and in a greater light, that multitude that no man can number, whose hope was in the Word made flesh, and with whom in the Lord Jesus we are for ever one.
>
> These prayers and praises let us humbly offer up to the Throne of Heaven, in the words which Christ himself hath taught us.[2]

The service itself, amended significantly in 1919, with its familiar passages from Scripture and a variety of carols, old and new, is indissolubly associated with King's College, Cambridge, and its choral worship. It also became a part of the English national narrative. For many subsequent

---

2   Routley, *The English Carol*, pp. 248–9.

generations, it marked the beginning of Christmas. Broadcast first in 1928, it could only achieve its iconic status by the spread of the wireless, deepening family connections across the Empire and Commonwealth (as well as in the United States), and similarly by the shared experience of international conflict during the Second World War.

Milner's vision has elements that would have resonated with (Sir) John Reith on his joining the British Broadcasting Company (sic) in 1922 in terms of creating a national, international, impartial, and high-quality broadcasting network. Milner quickly established the link, with the first broadcast from King's Chapel coming in 1926. From Reith's perspective, the regular weekly broadcast of *Choral Evensong* on the Home Service, its longest-running radio series, and usually coming from a cathedral or college chapel along with its choir, was completely aligned with Milner's own feelings about English public worship more widely. The Christmas Eve service has become so familiar that its skill as an importantly public act of worship can be overlooked. The musical scholar Benji Stegner has recently pointed out that one of its elements is a balanced intergenerational participation, as well as that between clergy and laity, civic and ecclesiastical.[3] Milner followed the Christmas Eve service with an Advent service in 1934 and a later one for Epiphany at York Minster in 1947, thereby enriching the familiar pattern of the Christian year. Not regularly broadcast in the same way, the Advent carol service, which some view as superior liturgically, has become a regular feature of many cathedrals and large churches. For college chapels, the Advent service has the advantage of being in term.

These non-mandatory acts of worship and dedication, both within the scriptural Kalendar and more widely, did not develop in a post-1918 vacuum, having origins before 1914, and evolving more broadly within civic worshipful acts. Usually held in cathedrals or large churches, across the year, they were not exclusively linked to the main Christian festivals and "Red Letter" days. Even before 1914, cathedrals regularly "hosted" performances of Handel's *Messiah*, Mendelssohn's *Elijah*, and the Bach *Passions*, for example, usually responding to local choral and other

---

[3]   Benji Stegner, "For He is our Childhood's Pattern: Nine Lessons and Carols as an Intergenerational Model", *The Choral Journal* 60:5 (2019), pp. 10–19.

societies' need for a spacious venue. But they were increasingly combined with national anniversaries, civic ceremonies, and opportunities for voluntary charitable bodies to come together and affirm in public what they do and what they represent—Remembrance Sunday, the beginning of the mayoral or judicial year, rededications of service organizations, whether military, civil, or voluntary, are examples.[4]

A college character and the chapel community

As far as his residential life in King's as an unmarried don was concerned, the college retained much of its self-conscious image, nurtured before 1914, as an informal, liberal place with a reputation in the arts. But there was a change in emphasis among the undergraduates, best seen in their magazine, *Basileon*. Founded in 1900, it had had a literary emphasis before 1914 with youthful contributions from E. M. Forster and Rupert Brooke, among others. After 1918, it took on a benignly satirical character, featuring individual dons, college societies and events. Milner frequently featured in his role as dean in limericks, cartoons, and surreal happenings. Nor is this surprising. He was very recognizable as an Anglo-Catholic dean by the style of his clerical dress, his distinctive voice, and his personal foibles, including crippling silences.

By contrast, his presiding style at the choir's summer camps, run on modified Scout lines at Batcombe, Somerset, revealed a different side of his personality. Photographs show him in a tweedy version of a Scoutmaster's uniform, but instead of the common names for Boy Scout troop or Wolf Cub pack leaders such as Skipper or Akela, Milner invented more Anglican versions, with himself as Arch. His weekly teaching of divinity in King's College School revealed a different man, remembered fondly 40 years later by Michael Ramsey and others.[5] He was often known

---

4   Civic services—examples below during Milner's time at York, see Special Services YML 1955, Book 3.

5   Mary Holtby, "Childhood Memories of Eric Milner-White", in Holtby (ed.), *Eric Milner-White: A Memorial*, pp. 43–5; Michael Ramsey, "Epilogue", Pare and Harris, *Milner-White: A Memoir*, pp. 93–106.

formally as Father Milner-White DSO at this time, which drew attention to his gallantry award that even the most religiously sceptical dons or undergraduates could not fail to respect.

A particular focus for Milner was the development of the chapel community, with dean's breakfasts and informal gatherings in his rooms, as well as the nurturing of those who might be considering ordination, along with a strong encouragement to train at Cuddesdon. As a historian dean, he does not seem to have engaged in the college's tutorial teaching, although he gave faculty lectures on "The Renaissance in England".

But, among undergraduates, it was *Basileon* that best conveys how Milner was regarded within the college.

Here are some examples:

> A spoof notice of a forthcoming new play, "Vive L'Enterprise", in whose first scene "Rev. Milner-White and his coterie have promised to appear as The Twelve Plagues of Egypt" (1925).

> Or another "Spoof Elegy in a Suburban Churchyard" with Milner introduced through "The wheezy call of the incense breathing Dean", and in a later edition as "Breathless with adoration" (1928).

Finally, in a series of clerihews:

> Milner-White
> looks well by candle light
> That's why,
> We have our services high. (1928)[6]

We have almost no knowledge other than that provided by Wilkinson, himself an undergraduate and later a Fellow from the late 1920s, of how Milner thought of himself as a college figure. But possibly there is some clue in his last sermon, specifically addressed to those who had arrived in the previous few weeks, on 19 October 1941 (Founder's Day) in the

---

6   KCAC *Basileon*.

middle of the war, in which he chooses the four beauties that mark the college, continuing,

> And here let me say a word to the youngest Kingsmen among us ... the best thing you can, each and all, give to the world is *a beautiful character.*[7]

As far as the dons and college affairs were concerned, the chapel was largely left to him, with Milner negotiating the various interests with care, especially in relation to the music and choir under the long-serving "Daddy" Mann, with new work introduced gently to include "modern" works by Stanford and Parry and, less enthusiastically for Mann, Vaughan Williams and Howells.[8] Similarly, modest changes were made in chapel liturgy, only slowly rebalancing the pattern of Sunday worship of litany and Matins, and through a more frequent celebration of the Eucharist including weekdays, along with supplementary prayers. Most of Milner's writing and publishing of prayers in the 1920s was directed towards college and school chapel services or other clerical institutions. The rejection of the 1928 Prayer Book prompted him to turn his attention to enhancing the liturgical structure of the BCP's most popular services, culminating in *Beyond the Third Collect*, and including special services.[9]

As examples, Milner had earlier written with Charles Wood, the master of the choristers at Gonville and Caius, *The Passion according to Mark* (1920), deploying fewer vocal and musical resources for parish and

---

[7] KCAC, Modern Archives/EMW/1/36. I would like to thank Tom Davies, Assistant Archivist, King's College, Cambridge, for finding this text for me. I discovered subsequently that it had been published as Eric Milner-White, *King's College, Cambridge: a sermon preached in the Chapel on Sunday 19th October 1941, in the quincentenary year* (King's College, Cambridge, 1941); BL ref. 4481.b.2.

[8] Wilkinson, *Milner-White*, p. 15.

[9] Among many writings on Prayer Book revision, Milner wrote two in the Cambridge academic journal *Theology*, in 1920 and 1943: Milner-White, "Prayer Book Revision", *Theology* Vol. I/3 (September 1920), pp. 123–34, and Vol. XLVI/280 (October 1943), pp. 217–24.

smaller collegiate use. He also published *Cambridge Offices and Orisons* (1921) in collaboration with B. T. D. Smith, Dean of Sidney Sussex, to improve liturgies in college chapels and schools as well as in Anglican fraternities and brotherhoods. These were for use in the daily offices of Terce, Sept, and None, work akin to his later exhaustive reworking of the *Cuddesdon Office Book* in 1940.[10]

These changes were not confined to King's. Many of the young Anglo-Catholic priests, appointed pre-war, returned to both Cambridge and Oxford after 1918, continuing their ministry, supplemented by their own experience as army chaplains—the Revd T. W. Pym (Dean of Trinity, Cambridge) and the Revd F. R. Barry (Fellow of Oriel College, Oxford) are two examples, both of whom had also won the DSO. What this meant in practice was an increase in the sacramental character of worship in college chapels, so it was reported in 1928 that many colleges now had both a Sunday and a weekday Eucharist, daily in five cases—King's, Trinity, Gonville and Caius, Sidney Sussex, and Pembroke.[11]

As for the chapel building itself, Milner did not take an intense interest in the fabric, which was also true later at York. But an engagement with glass, decoration, furnishing, and memorials was inevitable. These included the dedicated chapels to former members killed in the Great War, including at King's a new panel dedicated to Milner's great friend at Harrow and King's, Captain Gerald Fitzgerald.[12]

The case of the Fitzgerald window is interesting as the first of two examples in this period of Milner creating new windows as distinct from repairing or restoring existing historic stained glass. At King's, Milner sought out "spare" college glass or acquired other appropriate

---

[10]   Wilkinson, *Milner-White*, pp. 12–16.

[11]   Cambridge collegiate worship is discussed by Milner in 1927 and 1928 in the *Church Times*, 6 May 1927, p. 533 and 18 October 1928, p. 656.

[12]   Gerald Thomas Fitzgerald (1883–1915), Harrow and King's College (1903–6), read history and shared rooms with Milner. Later a barrister, he enlisted in 1914 in the Durham Light Infantry and was killed at Armentières on 30 December 1915. Fitzgerald's father was also a practising lawyer, and it seems likely that the fathers were friends. Milner's younger brother, Rudolph, married Fitzgerald's sister, Geraldine, in 1922.

historic glass, which drew attention to the historic Essex background of the Fitzgerald family. The composition of the new window was artfully constructed so that the light transferred at certain times onto the person memorialized.[13] This was also the case in the newly built parish church at Bitterne, Southampton, Milner's childhood home, dedicated to the memory of his father, Sir Henry Milner-White, following his death in 1922. In this case, Milner was part of a collaborating team, but it is reasonable to assume that his voice was strong about the glass, which was a combination of scriptural stories and civic historical reminders.[14]

This early thinking about "new" glass can later be seen in the guidance Milner wrote for donors and parish and diocesan bodies in the 1950s.

Milner's other main contribution to the university's religious life during the 1920s was the foundation of the Oratory of the Good Shepherd, formally inaugurated on 25 October 1919, with the opening of Oratory House on 24 June 1920 in the influential presence of William Temple (shortly to become Bishop of Manchester), Charles Gore (recently retired Bishop of Oxford), Edward Wood (later Earl Halifax, Viceroy of India, and Foreign Secretary), Bishop Weston of Zanzibar, and the young scientist Joseph Needham.[15]

As we have seen earlier, the idea of a Cambridge non-collegiate Anglican centre had taken preliminary shape and outline before Milner returned to King's in 1912, but much that had been achieved over the next two years had stalled with the outbreak of war. Initially it had been inspired by John How among the new college deans, anxious to create an inter-collegiate fraternity of Cambridge deans, chaplains, and committed

---

[13] Milner-White, Eric, as an appendix to M. R. James, *A guide to the windows of King's College, Cambridge* (Cambridge: Cambridge University Press, 1930).

[14] The Church of the Ascension, Bitterne, Southampton, see Nicholas Pevsner and David Lloyd, *The Buildings of England: Hampshire and the Isle of Wight* (London: Penguin Books, 1967), pp. 590–2; Bitterne Local History Society, <https://bitterne.net>; <http://sotonopedia.wikidot.com/> (accessed 1 November 2024); YML, Special Collections 59–2-22/23—Two folders of original photos of the glass and memorials in the church, with dedications, almost certainly by Milner.

[15] Tibbatts, *Oratory*, pp. 31–6.

Anglo-Catholic dons. John How, a serious and earnest man, recognized that Milner's different talents had provided the energy and "vision" for the project since his return to Cambridge in 1912, but this had been lost since August 1914. From 1917, he was encouraging the university and Milner himself to bring about a return to Cambridge as soon as possible.[16]

A complex story led in October 1919 to the establishment of the only Anglican oratory in the UK, with Milner becoming its Superior a few months later—a post he held until resigning in 1938, and from the Oratory completely the following year. The Oratory survives today as a "fraternity" with a core of Anglican celibate priests across the Anglican Communion with some 30 fully admitted members, but unsurprisingly in a form different from the founders' ambitions and aspirations.[17]

Alan Pigott chronicles what became the rather tense relations between Milner and some of the newer members of the Oratory in the 1930s regarding its direction, most notably with Alec Vidler, himself a later Dean of King's. In part this was due to what Pigott calls Milner's "perfectionism" and reluctance to adapt to the changing complexion and character of the Anglo-Catholic priesthood.[18]

Internally, those ancient wounds among the members are still felt, as is shown in "The Founder who we need not have lost . . . "[19]

For our purposes, what did this "perfectionism" involve? It is an ambiguous concept. At one level, it can be a personal and unconstructive stubbornness in matters of detail. At another, it can be an inspiring

---

[16]   George Tibbatts, *John How*, provides considerable detail on the origins of the OGS.

[17]   In 2024, there are just over 30 fully dedicated celibate Anglican priests, as members of the Oratory, to which should be added Companions, who can be both men and women and not committed to celibacy. Figures provided in the *Anglican Religious Life Yearbook* (accessible online). The Oratory has produced two histories by Henry Brandreth in 1958, brought up to date by George Tibbatts in 1988.

[18]   Pigott, Oxford DPhil.

[19]   Father Gregory, "Eric Milner-White: The Founder we need not have lost?" (London: The Oratory of the Good Shepherd, Province of Europe—Oratory Life, 2017).

vision, determinedly adhered to, despite the shifting sands of social and cultural change. Both elements had their place in Milner's thinking, which explains his alienation from the Oratory in the later 1930s. Those tensions and their uncomfortable resolution over time also paradoxically explain why the Oratory survived, when so many styles of Anglican vocation, flowing out from the Oxford Movement, have found themselves marooned on a fast-eroding sandbank, of which the Cowley Fathers in Oxford is a good recent example. Why then has the Oratory of the Good Shepherd survived?[20]

In a relatively short study of a complex man's personality and career, there can only be broad-brushstroke explanations.

Taking Oratorian ideals, it is probably true that Oratorians live under the most general of religious rules. As developed for an Anglican priest, Milner wrote an exposition of its ideals in 1918, and later its Seven Rules; both much discussed, these were lighter still. It was to be a body of celibate priests, who agreed to work within a spiritual "framework" as distinct from a more disciplined rule. This had implications in relation to what was expected from its members. For instance, poverty was not required, but a financial contribution to the "common" funds was expected.[21]

Alongside these personal commitments, there were other assumptions which made this Anglican version of the Oratorian ideal very difficult to ground, especially that of priestly celibacy and mission. More important was Milner's assumption that the order should continue to be closely connected with the University of Cambridge—spiritually, theologically, and geographically—reflecting as it did in the pre-1914 thinking of How and others in relation to the non-collegiate institutions. Cambridge was to remain the Oratory's physical and operational "home". Pusey House had never been intended to act in the same way. Better funded, it was a Christian residential centre of scholarship and learning, with a negotiated relationship with the university, enabling it to have undergraduate

---

[20]   Cowley Fathers, see Chapter 4, footnote 16 above.

[21]   The 1918 text of the ideals is substantially reproduced in Michael Ramsey's epilogue to Pare and Harris, *Milner-White: A Memoir*, which is included as an appendix in that volume, pp. 94–6. (Reprinted as an appendix in this volume, pp. 166–76 below.)

residents and authorized tutors, also replicated by the Benedictine St Benet's Hall for the Roman Catholic community. Furthermore, the Oratory had no formal connection with Anglican ordinand training, as was possible in Oxford at Cuddesdon and St Stephen's House. Nor did the Oratory have other than informal links with Westcott House or with one of the fully established colleges, as was the case with Keble in Oxford. From its very beginning, the OGS faced the dilemma of where its centre needed to be located, and what its functions and mission should be.

On the other hand, an Oratorian model did have advantages, especially as interpreted through its Rule in the very different circumstances after 1918. Very crudely, the spread of the spirit of the Oxford Movement after 1845 was a very English-centred priestly, parochial, social, and liturgical development within a church also engaged in missionary conversion overseas. The Church itself had been consumed by tensions over theology and scientific advance, denominational rivalry, and vexatious ritualist rows at home after 1870, along with the continuing anomaly of being an established church within two of the "historic" nations that made up the Union of Great Britain and Ireland (England and Wales) from 1801.

By the mid-1920s, the position of the Anglican Church was very different at home and overseas within the English-speaking world, especially the Empire. The ritualistic and Romish rows had died down and were now partially controlled, the challenge of the Nonconformist churches less feared, and only in England was the Church of England still established. Furthermore, the activities of the Church of England overseas had become a mixture of fraternal relations in the main among the Dominions, and more educational and medical than missionary within the colonies. Among these imperial and colonial territories, the Anglican Church was not "established". But the reliance on English ordained priests, especially in Africa, was still critical, and an attractive vocation for many young men and women, both secular and religious, for whom England remained "home". With a more globally scattered clergy, the need for more dispersed clerical fraternities also evolved, using the improvements in communication through the wireless and travel, and of which there was evidence from Africa as early as 1916.[22]

---

[22] Tibbatts, *Oratory*, p. 11.

By the mid-1930s, these challenges became increasingly painful for Milner, especially at the periodic gatherings of the whole membership, with the result that he resigned as the Superior in 1938 and from the order completely a year later. In some ways, this crisis was the saving of the concept of a distinctive Anglican Oratory with a more dispersed nature, no longer dominated by its Cambridge origins and without a fixed residential house. It had become more a fraternity of celibate Anglican priests, engaged mainly in parochial ministry across the Anglican Communion. It has since remained formally presided over, as the Visitor of the Oratory, by a leading figure within the Church, of whom the most well known have been Archbishops Ramsey and Williams.[23]

---

[23] Tibbatts, *Oratory*, pp. 37–59.

8

Beyond Cambridge

Reform of the Prayer Book and the writer of prayers

In the general optimism immediately following the Armistice, the hope among Anglo-Catholics was that there was the potential for a new "renaissance". Clearly this was a mood affecting Milner as he adjusted to a very different world, following from his own experiences since 1914. He was no different from any other combatant, from the ordinary soldier or citizen as well as any officer, however senior. For Milner in picking up the pieces in the same place, King's College, was how he would respond to the unfinished business of 1914, and how that might be refashioned in 1918.

One element in this was to continue work on a new and authorized Book of Common Prayer and to secure the approval of Parliament through the Church's own deliberative structures. As far as Cambridge was concerned, a group of priests and dons decided to found a new academic journal, originally entitled *Theology: A Journal of Historic Christianity*, but quickly amended to simply *Theology*, in the first issue of which in 1920, Milner contributed an article on "Prayer Book Revision".[1] But he did not become a central figure in the evolution of the 1927/8 Prayer Books, both of which were rejected by Parliament.

In terms of his writing on liturgy and prayers in the 1920s, Milner focussed on collegiate worship in schools, colleges of all sorts, and larger parochial centres of worship, all of which needed an appropriate

---

[1]   Eric Milner-White, "Prayer Book Revision", *Theology* Vol. I (September 1920), pp. 123–34. For comparison, *Theology* Vol. XLVI (October 1943), pp. 217–24.

liturgy—words, prayers, music, hymns, and homily, as he had highlighted in *The Church in the Furnace*.

It was therefore reasonable to take the BCP as a touchstone for such developments. Milner's own prayers and liturgies reflect that—*Cambridge Offices and Orisons* (1921), with Bertram Smith, Dean of Sidney Sussex, *The Occasional Papers of the 1928 Prayer Book Reconsidered, Memorials upon Several Occasion* (1933), later supplemented and republished as *After the Third Collect* (1952), *The Cambridge Bede Book* (1936) and *The Cuddesdon Office Book* (1940), anonymous but effectively a collaboration between Milner and the then Principal, Eric Graham, are the evidence of this.

The final rejection of the 1928 Prayer Book was a humiliation that stymied general liturgical reform for 30 years until Archbishops Fisher and Ramsey re-established the Liturgical Commission in 1955, of which Milner as Dean of York was a member.

Paradoxically, the 1928 rejection may have proved creative as well as distressing since it restored the status quo ante, which all knew was unsatisfactory, thereby allowing not fully authorized practices to continue and develop. Whereas, if there had been a new fully authorized canon, it would have required compliance. It allowed, if only by accident, individual writers of prayers to exercise their talents and enable the results of their creativity to be used unofficially.

In many ways, Milner's most influential contribution to the revision of the BCP was a result of the rejection of the 1928 Prayer Book through his own revision of the prayers proposed in that rejected Prayer Book, plus the addition of prayers that could be authorized without parliamentary consent for use within the BCP. The ultimate summation of this was expressed in the significantly titled *After the Third Collect* (1952). This collection took in many cases familiar prayers, not officially authorized, as supplements to the regular authorized structure of the BCP, modified modestly in the tone and language of 1662. They became so familiar from the 1930s in regular worship across the Christian year and for special services that most worshippers would not have known their more recent pedigree. Among these, to give a single important example, is "Drake's Prayer", which is Milner's rendering of a short passage in one of Sir Francis Drake's private letters on the day he sailed into Cadiz in 1587.

The two versions of this prayer written by Milner for the National Days of Prayer on 26 May 1940 and on 23 March 1941, and prior to D-Day on 6 June 1944, were used widely, both then and subsequently:

> O Lord God,
> when thou givest to thy servants
> to endeavour in any great matter,
> grant us also to know that it is not the beginning,
> but the continuing of the same unto the end,
> until it be thoroughly finished, which yieldeth the true glory;
> through him who for the finishing of thy work,
> laid down his life, our Redeemer, Jesus Christ.[2]

What this illustrates, as in so many ways, is that the state's unwritten constitution as well as that of its established Church "bumbled along" responding to external changes in behaviour and attitude permeating practice in an evolutionary manner—simultaneously creative, unsatisfactory, at times both complacent and realistic.

Milner's style and approach was later seen as anachronistic, especially in a worshipping environment that increasingly valued greater freedom of expression. But two points can be made here. First, that Milner was usually asked to write in the mode of the BCP, even if this was probably also his own preference. Second, it ignores the significance of the BCP in the Anglo-Catholic tradition, which recognizes ancient strands of adoration, humility, forgiveness, and exaltation in earlier worship, subsequently incorporated into Cranmer's original texts, which was not intended (in the eyes of Anglo-Catholics at least) to be radical. Rather more it was seen as a significant development within the English

---

[2] For "Drake's Prayer", see Philip Williamson, Stephen Taylor, Alasdair Raffe and Natalie Mears (eds), *National Days of Prayer: Special Worship since the Reformation, Vol. 3: Worship for National and Royal Occasions in the United Kingdom, 1871 to 2016*, Church of England Record Society Vol. 26 (Woodbridge: Boydell & Brewer, 2020), pp. 406–21. For a fuller treatment of Milner's contribution to the wartime National Days of Prayer, see below, Chapter 10.

catholic tradition of evolution and renewal at the same time as, but not fully determined by, changing political and religious circumstances in parochial practice around the English-speaking world.

The BCP is, obviously, not only an authorized handbook for regular weekly parish worship; it is also the core text for all Anglican services and offices, including critically the Eucharist, baptism, confirmation, burial, and ordination. Within this structure is the Kalendar of the Anglican Christian Year, including the commemoration of the Virgin, the saints and martyrs, and the important Christian seasons, most notably Holy Week and Christmas. In addition, the decades between the wars witnessed a growing national and civic demand for special services bringing together not only regularly practising Anglicans, but other communities, for collective worship in a large church building, usually an Anglican church or cathedral, acting as the Church Established under Law.

Armistice Day and the associated Sunday are obvious examples, as was the later version of the original Empire Day, which after 1945 became the less controversial and more inclusive Commonwealth Sunday, as well as more specific Anglican special services, such as those for the Mothers' Union or the Church of England Men's Society. Interdenominational bodies like the Boy Scouts gradually developed a celebration and rededication Sunday near St George's Day (23 April), a practice later affirmed by their patron, George V, and his successors. Uniformed workers—representing nursing and first aid organizations, women's voluntary services, professional and other voluntary bodies—wished for the occasional special service. Many mayor-making days often included both a civic parade and a church service. Particularly significant for this story were the National Days of Prayer developed during and after the First World War, a strangely symptomatic development in the continuing evolution of relations between the Established Church and the State.

In reviewing Milner's volumes of prayer and in his addresses and other writings in this period, it is important to remember that they are the product of a particular clerical education, anchored in the experiences of a group of Anglo-Catholic priests in Cambridge before 1914. Their dissatisfaction was with the restricted pattern of worship in the Church of England in parishes and places of education, which saw worship as a "Sunday only experience" of Matins and evensong with hymns and a

sermon, rather than realizing the full potential offered within the structure
and spirit of the Book of Common Prayer. For them, worship needed
to return to being a more sacramental journey as part of the annual
pattern of Christian living and prayer, with less emphasis on human
sin, repentance, and exhortation. Central to this was a regular Eucharist
at a more approachable hour for ordinary parishioners and students,
a greater appreciation of the Christian year, especially Holy Week,
and a recognition of special days and occasions within that Kalendar.
Milner played a significant part in what proved to be a transformation
in Anglican practice from the 1930s within parishes as well as in great
churches and chapels, as he reflected in his valedictory address to the
Church Union in 1962, quoting the Parish Communion Movement as
one example.[3]

Anti-papalism and ecumenism

The final element that I want to consider in relation to Milner's church
life during the 1920s is his attitude to the Roman Catholic Church and
ecumenical relations within Christian churches worldwide, the subject
of his address at the first Anglo-Catholic Congress in 1920. One of the

---

[3]   There is little comprehensive analysis of Milner's talent for writing prayers,
      except a paper delivered to the Friends of York Minster and reprinted in
      their 1984 annual report by Adrian Leak, pp. 18–23. The Revd Adrian Leak
      (b.1938) was Archivist and Vicar Choral at York Minster from 1981–6. What
      is less widely known is that Milner was asked to contribute to a volume,
      supported by the English Church Union, and published by the SPCK in 1932,
      edited by W. K. Lowther-Clarke, with the overall title of *Liturgy and Worship:
      A Companion to the Prayer Books of the Anglican Communion* (London:
      SPCK, 1932). Milner's contribution was entitled "Modern Prayers and their
      Writers", in which he discussed the development in Anglican liturgy and
      prayer following the Henritian break with Rome, and its history over the next
      three centuries, along with more recent developments since the Tractarians
      (Eric Milner-White, "Modern Prayers and their Writers", in Lowther-Clarke
      (ed.), *Liturgy and Worship*, pp. 749–62).

most public manifestations of the Anglo-Catholic enthusiasm of the years following 1918 were the periodic national Anglo-Catholic Congresses from 1920 until 1933. These were large gatherings in London and other provincial centres that combined high-profile lectures on Anglo-Catholic themes with processions, acts of collective worship and evangelism. Reports on their proceedings were published in addition to extensive press coverage. Milner addressed and participated in all of them, usually on the universality of the catholic faith and the barriers to an understanding of that.[4]

Part of the immediate post-war confidence was in terms of possible reconciliation and convergence within the catholic churches across the Christian world, through an emphasis on areas of common history and tradition along with what Milner called a "mystical union" of catholic understanding. Such a notion was always too grandiose for ecumenical relations at the time, as Anglo-Catholics themselves demonstrated through their published objections to the Mansfield Manifesto in April 1920 on the possible reconciliation between Anglicans and Methodists/Nonconformists.[5] Milner's prime concern was always with the contemporary Roman Catholic Church, and especially its own development since 1870, as we have already seen before 1914. It was one of his weaknesses that he had little or no interest in, or understanding of, the English (or indeed the European) reformed tradition, except through its more extensive composition and use of hymns from the late seventeenth century, itself an earlier Lutheran innovation.[6]

His two significant contributions to these questions were to the multi-authored *Essays: Catholic and Critical* (1926) and *One God and Father of All* (1929) (co-authored by fellow OSG founder and the Warden of

---

4   William Davidge, "The Congress Movement: The High Watermark of the Oxford Movement", in Stewart J. Brown, Peter B. Nockles and James Pereiro (eds), *The Oxford Handbook of the Oxford Movement* (Oxford: Clarendon Press, 2017), pp. 517–29.

5   Anglo-Catholic response to the Mansfield Manifesto, *Church Times*, 16 April 1920, p. 389.

6   Natalie Watson has helpfully reminded me that the BCP does not include the singing of hymns.

Oratory House, Father Wilfred Knox), which was a riposte to Father Vernon Johnson's *One Lord, One Faith* (1929), following Johnson's conversion to Roman Catholicism.[7]

Both are stridently, if differently, expressed in anti-papal terms, particularly in Rome's denial of the legitimacy of Anglican orders and its general hostility to Modernism. Both are detailed and complex, and only a few of their themes can briefly be described.

In *Essays: Catholic and Critical*, Milner wrote on "The Spirit of the Church in History", using the phrase the "Global Spirit of the Church". Both titles have echoes of the late philosophical idealism that, as mentioned earlier, had been so popularly dominant in English educated thinking and culture before 1914, including its emphasis on the "dialectic" in human history. In this reading, the Christian faith was the most developed of the Hebraic faiths through its progressive momentum in contrast to the "static" character of Islam, and what among other faiths he called the "retrogradism" of Buddhism. (Echoes here of his hostile votes in Browning's Political Society as an undergraduate between 1903 and 1906.) Once again, the blind spots were obvious at the time and more so later. First, peculiar in a historian, is his apparent belief that Christian missionary endeavour had been wholly by persuasion. Second, such a perspective is at odds with the fact that two of his closest undergraduate friends at King's, Philip Loyd and Douglas Hill, were both working at the time in India as a bishop or college principal. On the other hand, Milner presented the positive elements in Anglo-Catholicism as being undermined by the "regimentation" of the Church of Rome, "now governing disastrously", weakening its function "as the trustee for all Christendom of the religion of Christ".

Given Milner's robust tone in the essay, it will come as no surprise that he seems to have had nothing to do with the informal conversations at Malines from 1921 to 1927 or with any of Viscount Halifax's efforts

---

7   Eric Milner-White, "The Spirit of the Church in History", in Gordon Selwyn (ed.), *Essays: Catholic and Critical* (London: SPCK, 1926), pp. 322–42. This volume is one of the most significant Anglo-Catholic collections of writings in the interwar period, in many ways similar in its impact to that of *Lux Mundi* in 1889.

through his leadership of the English Church Union (of which Milner was an active member) to open dialogue with Rome.[8] Nor, as far as we know, did he associate with the growth of the community of those committed to the shrine at Walsingham, and certainly not the new European centres of Roman Catholic devotion and healing at Lourdes and Lisieux. Milner obviously supported the growth of Anglican celibate priestly orders, and was probably involved in the evolution of the Anglican Franciscans, ultimately based at Hilfield in Dorset. However, Little Gidding was never seen by members of the OGS as a shrine, more as a place of historical inspiration and retreat for its clerical members. It was more akin to the village of Tolpuddle in Dorset for the British Labour movement than a popular "holy" site. Later in the 1930s and after the Second World War, Milner did support the idea of memorializing "officially" the heroes of the post-Reformation Anglican Church from both the seventeenth and nineteenth centuries and was later asked by the two archbishops in 1948 to chair a group to research the question.

If his contribution to *Essays: Catholic and Critical* was "strong beer", *One God and Father of All: A Reply to Father Vernon* (1929) was neat spirit. Written with Father Wilfred Knox, it was in a sense the OGS reply to the claims of Rome as expressed through Father Vernon's own account, in *One Lord, One Faith*, of his conversion following a trip to Lisieux and a meeting with St Thérèse's blood sisters. This was a work described by the anonymous reviewer in the *Church Times* as being of "astonishing naivety", and it prompted a rapid response by Milner and Father Knox.[9]

In what can be only a short summary, the tone is set from the outset. Its explicit aim is to challenge the "exclusive" claims of the Roman Church within the three catholic traditions and to "infallibility", either logically or historically. The present Roman Catholic Church had had, in the authors' view, an "impaired catholic character" since 1870 in its attitude to the "advance of new knowledge and progress of scholarship", both in the sixteenth century and the nineteenth. In Father Vernon's hands, the

---

8   Malines Conversations, see Wikipedia.

9   Vernon Johnson, *One Lord, One Faith: An Explanation* (London: Sheed & Ward, 1929). The *Church Times* published an anonymous review on 25 October 1929, p. 495.

Church "is the Catholic Faith in its sixteenth-century expression plus the infallibility of the Pope" (pp. 1–20).

There follows an examination of the authority given by scripture and by the early Church to St Peter, including whether he ever reached Rome or how his charge by Christ "you are my rock" should be understood. For the two writers, the only "authority" for the Christian Church is in "the Person of our Lord", which includes elements of "private judgement, guided by the Holy Spirit" (p. 88).

The true catholic character of the Christian faith, they continue, is founded on the "value of the sacramental life, of the need for ordered ministry derived from the historic continuity of the episcopate from the Apostolic age, the tradition of mental prayer, and the belief in the living value of the communion of all the saints". The Church qua Church has the right to teach, but not to declare absolutely what is true, and the challenges of Modernism are not to be met by infallible declarations of dogma or truth (pp. 83–93).

In retrospect, it is quite difficult to understand the tone of the critique of Vernon Johnson's book. Johnson was a quite well-known Anglo-Catholic priest at the time, a popular preacher in the fashionable Anglo-Catholic churches of central London, Chairman of the Society of the Divine Passion, based in Essex, and slightly younger than Milner. He had been ordained in Chichester diocese in 1910–11 and was also very active in the Anglo-Catholic Congress movement after 1918, leading some of the regional congresses in the intervening years—in Nottingham and Manchester, along with one planned in Birmingham in 1929. Wilkinson describes him as a "friend" of Milner's. There may have been an element of personal betrayal in Milner's reaction to Johnson's conversion, following his instruction from Father C. C. Martindale. The role of Father Martindale may be significant here as one of a group of well-known Roman Catholic priests responsible for high-profile conversions in the period, including Wilfred Knox's own brother, Father Ronald Knox, who had so nearly converted the young Harold Macmillan in 1914.[10]

The *Church Times* did not rate the co-authored book very highly, describing the volume as "too Modernist" in tone, which is once again

---

[10]   On Father Vernon as friend, see Wilkinson, *Milner-White*, p. 27.

a contemporary comment on Milner's ecclesiology.[11] What it indirectly provides is the first relatively full account of what he regarded that doctrine to be, something which he only did fully in his short book, *Anglican Piety*, discussed earlier.

By 1930, there is evidence that the enthusiastic Anglo-Catholic optimism of the previous decade was waning, Anglo-Catholic Congresses were losing their focus, albeit continuing to be popular, and many minds were concentrated on the centenary of the Oxford Assize Sermon of 1833 and the associated Congress. At that event, it was decided that 1940 should be the date for the next Congress. In addition, it was becoming increasingly difficult to find the financial resources to support the ordination training of young Anglo-Catholic priests, with Milner making regular appeals on behalf of the Fiery Cross Association for donations.[12]

The temper of the age was also changing following the Wall Street Crash and the onset of the Great Depression, the rise of Hitler and the growth of Italian fascism as well as the concordat between Mussolini and the Vatican in 1929. Within the Empire, the rise of Indian nationalism and its acknowledgement by the British government was causing concern about the place of the Christian faith in a predominantly non-Christian subcontinent.

---

[11] *Church Times*, 18 December 1929, p. 741.

[12] The Fiery Cross Association was one of the smaller bodies linked to the (English) Church Union, raising funds to support the clerical training of Anglo-Catholic ordinands during the interwar years.

1: Harrow school boy

"O. B."

Scoutmaster's Heroism.

READS TO HIS BOYS WHILE DYING.

The Rev. Ernest Arthur Edghill, who, after an accident in which he received an injury which proved fatal, showed great fortitude by reading to his party of boy scouts in camp while awaiting medical aid.

3: Ernest Arthur Edghill, Milner's most important Southwark friend

2: Oscar Browning, Milner's tutor (opposite)

4: *Milner as a young priest, c.1910 (opposite)*

5: *Milner as army chaplain, no date*

6: Anglo-Catholic Congress, 1920; opening procession along Holborn, 29 June 1920

7: Milner as "Arch" in the Choristers' Camp, mid 1930s

8: Milner as Dean of York 1941–63

9: Hans Hess (1907–75), Curator, York City Art Gallery, c.1965

10: Philip Loyd (1884–1952), Trappist, lifelong friend, and bishop

12: Milner as York Minster restorer (opposite)

11: Arthur Michael Ramsey, Archbishop of York 1956–61 and Archbishop of Canterbury 1961–74

13: Milner, the collector of pots

15: Milner as elderly
Dean of York (opposite)

14: The Leaping Salmon 1931
by Bernard Leach (1887–
1979), City of York Art Gallery

9

A lacklustre decade, 1933–41

As far as Milner was concerned, these years before his departure to York in 1941 were the most barren of his career. The contrast with his near-contemporary William Temple was striking, despite their many shared religious principles, especially the late Victorian philosophical idealism that both had absorbed before 1914.[1]

More domestically, the anniversary of John Keble's Assize Sermon of 1833 was celebrated enthusiastically in both Oxford and London, with Milner preaching to a large gathering (estimated at 4,000) in the main quadrangle of Keble College to the theme "a very gallant regiment".[2] The year before, the Anglo-Catholic Congress movement had merged with the English Church Union (renamed as the Church Union), which sand-banked the Dean of King's within Cambridge. The regular pattern of college worship and the needs of undergraduates continued, and those contemplating ordination were nurtured, encouraged by Milner in the direction of Cuddesdon. At the same time, the OGS was experiencing structural, personal, and principled difficulties, distressing to Milner, and leading to his resignation as Superior and from the order itself in 1939.[3] Milner introduced an Advent carol service in 1934, and the choir went on its first overseas tour to Scandinavia in 1936. Among college chapels, the growth in weekday eucharists was commented on, as was the growth

---

[1]   William Temple (1881–1944): *ODNB*, vol. 54, pp. 90–5 (a sensitive article by Adrian Hastings).

[2]   *The Fifth Anglo-Catholic Congress, London and Oxford, 1933 in Commemoration of the Century of the Catholic Revival* (London: Loxley on behalf of the Anglo-Catholic Congress Committee, 1933).

[3]   Tibbatts, *Oratory*, pp. 51–4.

of the Anglo-Catholic Society (known as the Confraternity of the Holy Trinity), of which Milner was President, among undergraduates.[4]

Less locally, he completed his collection in 1933 of *Memorials on Several Occasions*, prayers and thanksgivings for public worship to supplement the services of the Book of Common Prayer, and a personal anthology of prayers, *The Cambridge Bede Book*, in 1936. At the same time, he was preparing a "perfectionist" definitive edition of the *Cuddesdon Office Book*.

Milner seems to have played almost no part or taken any interest in the two significant commissions preparing and reporting in the 1930s—that on Doctrine (1922–38) and that on Faith and Order (1938 and 1939) —both of which Temple chaired.

The one exception that the author has discovered is a Milner memorandum written to Bishop Headlam of Gloucester, who along with Temple was the leading bishop of the Church of England, participating in the work of the Faith and Order commission. Not significant itself in the slow deliberative processes leading to the founding of the World Council of Churches in 1948, it is an interesting statement of Milner's attitude to ecumenism ten years after the tensions of the 1920s. He begins by stating that any such process had to begin in prayer, creating a shared spiritual atmosphere and, by implication, not simply through multilateral negotiations on doctrine that had little influence on local practice, positively off-putting to regular worshippers. Within the liturgical sphere, he suggested that the use of the early church practice of agape could be helpful, in which Christians could come together in the breaking of bread and drinking of wine, followed by a simple communal meal and prayers without the elements being consecrated, as the recognition of Christ's injunction through his two commandments—to love God and to love one's neighbour as oneself—the highest form of love. How Milner had

---

4   The impact of the Anglo-Catholic Society (Confraternity of the Holy Trinity), with a reported membership of 120, on collegiate worship is discussed by Milner in 1927 and 1928 in the *Church Times*, 6 May 1927, p. 533; 18 October 1928, p. 656. The five named colleges where the Eucharist was celebrated daily were Gonville and Caius, King's, Trinity, Pembroke, and Sidney Sussex, in addition to Westcott House.

arrived at this understanding is not clear, although he states that this had been a continuing practice in the English medieval Church "up to the woeful change of religion". In the early eighteenth century, the Moravian Church adopted elements from within the agape tradition, which had a profound influence on John Wesley, and the later Methodist Church in the first half of the nineteenth century. Perhaps more plausibly, it was an echo of his closeness to Arthur Edghill between 1908 and 1912, given that Edghill not only lectured on modern theology, but also gave lectures on first-century Christian history at King's College, London. Since 1945, there has been a modest revival in agape, reflected in liturgical practice locally, through prayers for Christian unity, and weeks devoted to that ideal.[5]

Probably his most creative contribution to the Anglican Communion as a whole was within the columns of the *Church Times* about the designation of post-Reformation "heroes" as saints, whose lives could be celebrated liturgically within the Anglican churches in the Kalendar of Red Letter Days with appropriate biblical readings, collects, epistles and prayers. He also supported the idea of new churches having the opportunity to be dedicated to post-Reformation "heroes", as was the new John Keble Church, Mill Hill in north London in 1936, at the consecration of which Milner preached. These were questions that returned after 1945 and are discussed later.[6]

But this was, nevertheless, relatively small beer and Wilkinson hints that Milner had become stale and depressed, something later confirmed by Archbishop Ramsey.[7] Milner was 50 in 1934 and seemed to be going into comfortable middle age, career already accomplished. Whatever his mindset at this point, he declined to be considered for the deanery at

---

[5]   Agape—Lambeth Palace Library, Headlam Papers, MS2637 ff101–131— Memo 1939 from Milner on the ecumenical potential of the early church practice of agape. Archbishop Ramsey later commented on Milner's interest in Pare and Harris, *Milner-White: A Memoir*, p. 101.

[6]   Milner-White on post-Reformation saints, *Church Times*, 18 November 1927, p. 599; 9 May 1930, p. 593; 27 July 1937, p. 208.

[7]   Wilkinson, *Milner-White*, p. 36; Pare and Harris, *Milner-White: A Memoir*, p. 102.

Salisbury in 1936, with his situation remaining the same at the outbreak of the Second World War. With hindsight, his most useful experience in these years was his membership of the Ely Diocesan Advisory Committee, and his separate and critical report on its cathedral glass.[8]

One positive development during these years was that Milner had time and scope to extend his interest in the arts, theatre, and literature, in all of which he displayed an original, some would say idiosyncratic, engagement. The Fellows of King's were an artistic bunch with developed external connections in London, among whom were included Maynard Keynes and his wife, the ballet dancer Lydia Lopokova, "Dadie" Rylands, leading in the development of Cambridge theatre, Donald Beves, a "good College Fellow", independently wealthy with theatrical talents and a significant collection of Jacobean glass, and John Shepherd, classicist, director of Greek plays and subsequently Provost. E. M. Forster, now an established and renowned author, was a regular presence as the sympathetic biographer of G. Lowes Dickinson, who had died in 1932. Many were unmarried and lived in college. By this time, Milner was also a wealthy man, following the death of his father in 1922 and with the prospect of further inheritance. His main choice in collecting was that of twentieth-century Japanese ceramic pots, of which he was building up the most significant British collection in private hands by the 1950s (see below, Chapter 15).

He also avidly collected contemporary detective fiction, and from the early 1930s became an obsessive ballet goer. Later at York, he specialized in collecting heathers.

At some point, he became a friend (by his report) of Henry Morris (1889–1961), also a Kingsman, who as a slightly mature student had come to read philosophy in 1920, after giving up the idea of being ordained as a priest in the Church in Wales. Not a don, but the Director of Education for Cambridgeshire from the very early age of 33, he also had aesthetic interests in architecture, as reflected in his innovative village schools at Sawston, Impington, and elsewhere which had won him an international reputation. Unmarried, with a liking for the company of young men,

---

[8]   Milner-White report on the stained glass of Ely Cathedral 1938, YML, Pamphlets, Bay 10, Box 65/24.

he lived in central Cambridge, and like Charles Sayle before 1914, held soirees at his home. It was a connection that would later have an impact on the founding of the University of York.[9]

---

[9]   Henry Morris (1889–1961), *ODNB*, vol. 39, pp. 273–5; Harry Ree, *Educator Extraordinary: The Life and Achievement of Henry Morris, 1889–1961* (London: Longman, 1973); Tony Jeffs, *Henry Morris: Village Colleges, Community Education and the Ideal Order* (Nottingham: Heretics Press, 1998); Milner-White to Alfred Wayment, n.d., 1939, KCAC/Modern Archives/EMW/X/2/Wayment/1.

1 0

The move to York, 1940–1

In 1939, there was no reason why Milner should leave King's. He was 55 and had been Dean for 21 years. The outbreak of war made his lonely situation even more isolated, as King's emptied of dons and undergraduates. By May 1940, the country's situation was grim, with France about to fall, potentially trapping British forces around Dunkirk, coinciding with the collapse of the Chamberlain government. The elderly Archbishop of Canterbury, Cosmo Gordon Lang, thought the dire moment required a National Day of Prayer, building on earlier National Days of Prayer during the Great War and similar points of national danger in the following years. After preliminary soundings, it was decided that the most comprehensive, national, and imperial response, in Christian terms, was that such an announcement should be expressed as "the King's wish", that 26 May should be seen as a united national and imperial religious response to the situation in Europe. Such a "call to prayer" required both political and royal endorsement. Churchill, having only taken office a few days before, was not keen, but reluctantly agreed. The King was supportive and, among other things, agreed to make a broadcast to the Empire. The urgency implied rapid action from Lang. He turned to Milner to ask if he could provide a template for such a special service, along with additional prayers within the familiar Anglican parochial pattern of the Book of Common Prayer. Milner did this in short order, including writing many of the new prayers himself. But the template had to be constructed so that it could be adapted, if they wished, within other denominations and faiths, fulfilling the King's wish for a "National Day of Prayer". It also had to be of use across the Empire.

It secured widespread popular support and endorsement across the country, with well-attended services and a national service at St

Paul's attended by the King and Queen, Churchill, and the political establishment, replicated civically and locally. Churchill was impressed, changing his view about the importance of such national public religious responses, especially in June 1944 around D-Day, to which Milner also made a significant contribution.

It also showed again that Milner had a talent for creating special services at short notice, as in 1918. It is highly unlikely, in my opinion, that Churchill was unaware of Milner-White after May 1940. It was not so much that Churchill had anything like an explicitly religious response to the National Day of Prayer, it was more that it touched a deep chord in his sense of the "History of the English-Speaking Peoples"—such an ambiguous notion, but widely shared by his and Milner's generation.[1]

Not anticipated, the war had provided a way for Milner to break out of his Cambridge-centred clerical existence. It led to an unexpected result. In early 1941, Cosmo Gordon Lang faced a dilemma because he had a raft of interconnected appointments that needed Downing Street endorsement. It was a complex chess board of patronage, including that to the deanery at York, the most senior in the Northern Province. Dean Bate seemed to be in failing health and the York chapter were concerned. Canon Bell, as the senior chapter canon, had written to Lang on 8 June 1941, saying that the York chapter would probably need support if a vacancy occurred, and suggesting that Canon Milner-White might provide that element of vision required.[2] It was a risky suggestion as Milner had no previous diocesan or provincial experience, and had declined to be considered for the deanery of Salisbury, five years before. We do not know the full story, but Milner's name appeared on the potential shortlist with the result that his name was put forward from Downing Street to the Palace for endorsement. It may all have been left to the respective patronage secretaries, but I doubt it. Churchill would have known little of the others on the list, but it is likely that Milner's name would have become familiar

---

[1]   For Milner's major role in the wartime National Days of Prayer, see Williamson, Taylor, Raffe and Mears (eds), *National Prayers: Special Worship since the Reformation*, pp. 411–21.

[2]   Canon C. C. Bell to Archbishop Cosmo Gordon Lang, 8 June 1941, Lambeth Palace Library, Lang Mss, Vol. 182, ff. 251.

to him, if only recently. Milner was not a person anyone saw as a diocesan bishop, probably also his own opinion of himself. Given that Lang had received the opinion unsolicited from the York chapter, it gave him a steer, and it was a way of freeing up the chess board. It is also unlikely that Churchill did not know that Milner was a Harrovian, like himself.

Milner accepted immediately.

The city of York in 1941

York, of course, has been important since the Roman period, militarily, administratively, strategically, commercially, and ecclesiastically, especially after the adoption of Christianity by the Emperor Constantine in 312. These features had been confirmed in the following centuries as England consolidated and as the two provinces emerged within the Church, centred on Canterbury and York. Each had its archbishop and dioceses, exercising significant religious, social, economic, and political power. In addition, the city of York had prospered through the wool and cloth trades in the period following the Black Death from 1350 and was at the centre of royal government at the time of Edward III's wars against the Scots, as it was again during the English Civil War from 1642–4. While still an important regional city in the eighteenth century with a fashionably sociable culture, its commercial, manufacturing, and trading importance declined in contrast to the economic growth of the West Riding towns and cities. The reforms in church and state between 1780 and 1850 further reduced the significance of the city in the life of the nation, a feature shared by other cathedral cities such as Lincoln and Norwich. By the time of the Deans and Cathedrals Act 1840, York continued to exercise important responsibilities as part of the established Northern Province of the Church of England, but in a much more plural society, religiously and socially. But in a different cultural sense, York remained "the capital of Yorkshire".[3]

---

[3]   Patrick Nuttgens (ed.), *The History of York, Yorkshire: From the Earliest Times to the Year 2000* (Pickering: Blackthorn Press, 2001).

By mid-century, however, two external factors were to create the city of which Milner became the second citizen as dean in 1941. The first was the arrival of the railways, reaching York in 1840. By 1850, it provided the crucial connection to the North-East and Scotland, its status later visible in its grandiose headquarters on Tanner Row, combined with a major railway engineering centre at the Carriage Works, Leeman Road. The second was the growth of the confectionary trades with their focus on chocolate manufacture, and on two Quaker families—Rowntree and Terry—along with allied trades. The result was the rapid growth of working-class housing before 1914 for the railway staff around the works and South Bank, and for the chocolate workers at the new Rowntree factory complex on a 16-acre site on Haxby Road. Each had a distinctive employer/employee culture, with some common elements of corporate paternalism. In the case of the Rowntree family's Quaker inheritance, this led to high-level interest in housing and social conditions in York, as well as the creation of three variously named Rowntree trusts, with their emphasis on urban poverty and deprivation, most famously expressed in Seebohm Rowntree's *Poverty: A Study of Town Life* (1901). As a family and firm, they were unsurprisingly Liberal/Progressive in politics and prominently involved in civic life.

By 1941, these developments in the city had reached a maturity that would last throughout Milner's time as dean. As well as the Minster and many medieval city-centre churches, there was also a strong Methodist and Congregationalist presence in the city, as defined by their new churches, as well as a poor Irish Roman Catholic quarter along with a distinctive Quaker influence stretching back to the late eighteenth century, reinforced by confectionary production. Its civic politics was predominantly Liberal/Progressive and the influence of the Labour movement was modest given the city's working-class citizens. In parliamentary terms, however, the city continued to return Conservative members throughout the interwar years, except between 1929 and 1931.[4]

---

4   Patrick and Bridget Nuttgens, "Twentieth Century York", in Nuttgens (ed.), *The History of York*, pp. 302–55.

A cathedral city

As the incoming dean of a nationally and internationally significant cathedral, what system of governance did Milner inherit? Among ecclesiastical reforms during the nineteenth century, cathedrals with their deans and chapters were left largely untouched, unlike church schools, diocesan structures, the ancient universities and their colleges, and parochial church finances. They remained independent church corporations, attached to, but largely detached from, their bishop/archbishop and the local diocese/province. Their corporate structures remained historic and complex, which gave considerable flexibility and authority to the individual dean. Each incumbent could interpret his own ministry as dean—priest, scholar, builder, evangelist, moral reformer, or socialite. There was no age of retirement.

This freedom of interpretation of the role of a cathedral dean disguised a more fundamental question, appreciated at the time, of "what was the purpose of Anglican cathedrals in the mid-twentieth century?" This was the central issue of the annual Deans' Conference in 1943, for which the Dean of Lichfield, F. A. Iremonger, had written a report as the basis for discussion.[5] Milner attended the conference, and its papers are in the York Minster Library. Therefore, the question of what sort of dean he was to be was not just a personal one, especially for the second most important cathedral in the Church of England. It must have caused some trepidation among civic and church leaders alike. This was particularly the case in the middle of a global war, and in a diocese in which the archbishop's diocesan responsibilities were overshadowed by those of the province and wider church. Milner's knowledge of provincial civic life had largely ceased on going from Southampton to Harrow School in 1897. He had had little acquaintance with diocesan structures and lacked many of the relevant qualities to be either a bishop or a headmaster, as Patrick Wilkinson noted in 1963. Moreover, deans and their chapters were not the same as heads of house and Fellows of Oxbridge colleges.

---

5   YML, Milner-White MS/V/8, Papers of Deans' Conferences, 1935–63.

Being dean of a cathedral at this time was one of the most unusually untrammelled offices of church or state.[6]

In the event, Milner's interpretation of his role in church and city made him the most influential of the deans of York in the twentieth century. It was also transformative for him. As we will see later, his authoritative manner and the decisions about the Minster's medieval stained glass were not uncontroversial, but, by most criteria, his long tenure was a constructive success for the Minster, city, and wider church.

Milner, having accepted immediately and without any self-doubt, was admitted and installed a few months later, addressing his first full chapter in May 1942. What sort of dean was he going to be? It was difficult to predict. Milner seems to have drawn heavily on his family background, especially the experience of his father, Sir Henry Milner-White, as he had become in 1918, knighted for civic services in Southampton during the First World War. Sir Henry had been a prominent local businessman, a devout high churchman, with a public reputation within the town, county, and diocese. In York, his son, as the "second citizen", after the Lord Mayor, also had the opportunity to develop a civic voice, largely free of direct diocesan supervision. Milner grasped that opportunity with both hands, showing a skill, sensitivity, and creative enthusiasm for his newly adopted city. In this case, it was an ideal match as it played well to Milner's skills as a negotiator, exercising a considerable influence behind the scenes, as we shall see. These were in areas not political in a narrow sense, but broadly consistent with the aspirations expressed within the city in the early years of the war. Moreover, as Dean of York, he could provide "vision" for other English cathedrals. It was in great personal contrast to his colleague at Canterbury, Dean Hewlett Johnson, "the Red Dean", with his popularly expressed sympathy for the Soviet system throughout his long life.

---

[6]   G. R. Evans, *Crown, Mitre and People in the Nineteenth Century* (Cambridge: Cambridge University Press, 2021).

A civic dean

In 1942, there was modest scope for action until wartime restrictions eased. Even so, the city had high aspirations among leading councillors and citizens, which had been brought together by Alderman J. B. Morrell in a personal report in 1940, entitled *York: City of Our Dreams*. Morrell, a leading employer, philanthropist, and councillor, including having been Lord Mayor, wished the city to be "modern" in terms of business, employment, and as a provider of public services, but respectful of its remarkable history and heritage, with an urgent need for its preservation for contemporary purposes. Although very different in personality, talents, and religious practice, the two men complemented each other in their enthusiastic dedication to the city, especially in the arts, heritage, and architecture. Both respected each other's roles and the benefits of collaboration. Morrell quickly saw that Milner could be a great asset in realizing his vision for the city, inviting him to join the city council's newly formed civic committee in April 1942, and two months later to chair its culture subcommittee, which was given a wide remit.[7] Essentially, the civic committee was a working party attempting to map a future development of the city after the war, even though final victory was still three years away. With the publication of the Beveridge Report the following November, and a new Education Act anticipated, the civic atmosphere was one of reconstruction. Milner was re-energized, something noted by Michael Ramsey later, carefully involving himself in the schemes devoted to the art gallery, library, and museums, about which he could speak with expertise and authority. His subcommittee continued until the spring of 1944, with individual elected members preparing memoranda with recommendations on the future life of the city, including education, training, art and music, and Milner preparing a final concluding report in March 1944. With even less scope for new initiatives at the Minster, the civic committee had given Milner a speedy introduction to his newly adopted city and its principal citizens, councillors, and officers, as well

---

7   Katherine A. Webb, *City of our Dreams: J. B. Morrell and the Shaping of Modern York*, Borthwick Texts and Studies 44 (York: Borthwick Institute, 2019).

as to a range of public issues. As examples, after the Baedeker attack on the city on the night of 29 April 1942 and the destruction of the Guildhall and the nearby church of St Martin le Grand, Coney Street, Milner wrote a well-informed open letter to the Lord Mayor. Introducing himself, not explicitly as dean, but as a new citizen of the city, he urged the rebuilding of the historic church, rather than demolishing it totally and redeveloping the site. In an address to York's Rotary Club, a few weeks later, he endorsed the ambition to establish a university in the city. After completing his report to the civic committee in the spring of 1944, he actively supported the local opposition to the proposed construction of three additional cooling towers close to the historic centre, describing the scheme as a "monstrous erection".[8]

Alderman Morrell's principal civic ally at this time was Oliver Sheldon, an earlier senior executive of the Rowntree Cocoa Works and, by the late 1930s, active in conservation, preservation, and modernization in the city. An able and active man, with abilities as a creative promoter of the city, he had founded the York Georgian Society in 1939 with the remit "to promote the preservation and care, and to foster the study and appreciation of Georgian buildings in and around . . .". The two men were the civic energy among leading citizens, increasingly concerned for what the future might bring from 1942 onwards, once hostilities were over.[9]

Milner's concluding report of the work of his culture subcommittee to the main civic committee seems not to have survived. But a press cutting provides a summary. The report obviously had to provide comprehensive comment on the committee's work, not all of which would have engaged Milner personally. But the tone and vocabulary are distinctively his own.[10]

8   Eric Milner-White, "Open Letter to the Lord Mayor of York, 'Shall St Martin's, Coney Street be pulled down?'", YML, SC Pamphlets Box 120/24. On cooling towers, *Yorkshire Post*, 27 December 1944, p. 8.

9   Katherine A. Webb, *Oliver Sheldon and the Foundations of the University of York*, Borthwick Paper no. 115 (York: University of York, 2009).

10   York City Council, Civic Committee (1942–4), Milner-White's final Report as chairman of the Cultural Development subcommittee, scrapbook press cuttings, *Yorkshire Evening Press*, 8 March 1944. I owe this reference to Dr Katherine Webb.

Beginning at the highest level of aspiration, he stakes York's claim potentially to be a European city of significance, and on a par with other provincial European cities such as Florence and Venice. From this introduction, his report identifies ways forward in reconstructing the city, involving transport, buildings—historic, restored, and new— and how to approach its historic core. This would involve a mixture of iconic buildings, often churches, livery halls and others, as well as more domestic medieval structures, many in a very diminished state, a process that should be overseen by "neighbourhood" committees. Other buildings should be put to new use, especially the King's Manor and its site in the centre of the city, by relocating the Blind School (of which Milner was already Chairman), and redesignating the medieval buildings as a civic museum of "old York". In addition, there were proposals in relation to museums, galleries, and libraries, which probably engaged Milner more personally, as well as the building of a new civic centre.

In summary, the report provided a menu of aspirations for the variety of agencies that might contribute to decisions post-war. What it plausibly provided was an energizing element contributing to Oliver Sheldon's ambition that York should have its own civic trust and that the time was ripe.[11]

The end of the war in Europe in May 1945 provided that moment. A few months later, the York Civic Trust was formally created in early 1946 with Sheldon and Milner as its joint secretaries and Morrell as chairman.

Milner was certainly no longer simply "the new Dean".

Within this national and local post-war civic context, Milner identified most closely as joint secretary of the Civic Trust and Dean, in that order,

---

[11]   Civic trusts and preservation societies have their origins in the mid-nineteenth century as non-governmental voluntary (often charitable) community associations, dedicated to preserving and enhancing their local environment. They take many forms, and were given a national voice in 1959 with the founding of the Civic Trust—essentially an umbrella organization for its members. The national Civic Trust ceased operating in 2009, but the "Civic Trust" movement has been refashioned as Civic Voice, providing many of the support services of its predecessor. York Civic Trust was an early post-war example of its type and has played a significant role in the modern history of the city.

with the city's art gallery and the ambition to secure a university in York as priorities.

York City Art Gallery

In 1939, York City Art Gallery was a modestly successful provincial gallery, not dissimilar to the many established in the second half of the previous century. A local response to the general growth in urban civic pride and self-esteem and founded in 1879, it had relied on the philanthropy of its citizens to fund a building, as well as early legacies of personal collections or endowments. Milner's hometown of Southampton would be another example.

At the outbreak of war, there was nothing to suggest that the York gallery could raise its prestige or status to that of the great northern cities, a position not improved during the war, with part of the building requisitioned and another out of commission due to bomb damage. The one significant change was that the art gallery, along with museums and libraries, was a key element in Morrell's ambitions for the city of his dreams, as it was in Sheldon's commitment to the founding of a civic trust, in addition to its also being an important item for Milner's cultural subcommittee.[12]

After the war, Milner's active involvement in the gallery was as the long-serving chairman of the art gallery committee, as well as of the Art Gallery Society from 1949. With his existing position on the Civic Trust, Milner was a key figure in the post-war development of the gallery. His impact was threefold—his engagement in the appointment of a new curator, Hans Hess, coinciding with the gallery's reopening in 1948 and his continuing support of Hess until his own death in 1963, his active encouragement of the gallery's participation in the city's Festival of Britain in 1951, and most significantly through his personal generosity to its collections, following the death of his mother, also in 1951.[13]

---

[12]   Sarah Sheils, *The Friends of York Art Gallery: A Brief History* (York: Friends of York Art Gallery, 2017).

[13]   On Hans Hess, see Wikipedia entry.

A single example will have to suffice in each case. In appointing a new curator, Morrell and Milner drafted the job description. While he was not a member of the selection committee, Katherine Webb, the biographer of Morrell, is in little doubt about Milner's active involvement. Hess was a Jewish émigré from Germany in 1933 with interests in modern and contemporary German art. He was also a life-long Marxist, neither enthusiasm close to Milner's artistic or aesthetic tastes. Where they did converge, however, was in their passion for the place of the arts in a civilized society. Secondly, the opportunity to showcase the gallery for the Festival of Britain, with its focus on heritage and the arts, was actively pursued. It is worth remembering that Milner himself spoke at this time of cathedrals as a natural home for all the arts. Thirdly, Milner's own passion for collecting paintings and modern Japanese pioneer studio pottery, again a surprising choice (discussed below), was matched by his own increasing generosity to the city's gallery, replacing to a degree his earlier commitment to the Fitzwilliam Museum in Cambridge. In particular, the gifting of the bulk of his pot collection to the city art gallery raised its standing among English provincial galleries in ways that his other donations of individual pictures could hardly achieve. Milner's collection of pots provided a critical mass in York to an art form which could attract other similar donations, as it later did.[14]

The Civic Trust and the campaign for a university, 1947–63[15]

Milner had been very much the junior partner in the creation of the Civic Trust, although he had some knowledge of a somewhat similar body in Cambridge. Its early energizer continued to be Sheldon, with Milner writing the annual reports, which are the only surviving records

---

[14] Sarah Riddick, *Pioneer Studio Pottery* (see fn 4). Also, Helen Walsh, contribution to the 2016 Milner-White seminar on "What to look for in a pot".

[15] Allen Warren, *Eric James, and the Founding of the University of York*, Borthwick Paper no. 126 (York: Borthwick Institute for Archives, 2017).

of its early years. Progress was steady, with membership rising to 150 in 1947–8, with efforts mainly devoted to conservation issues. However, in that year there seemed to be an opportunity. Higher education had not been included in the 1944 Act and the post-war Percy and Barlow reports were not trying to plan for those future needs, once the school leaving age had been raised to 15, as it was in 1947.[16]

It is important to remember what was understood by a "university" at that time. Formally, it was an independent educational institution with degree-awarding powers of its own and governed by a charter from the Privy Council. If such an institution received central government money, it came directly in an annual allocation from the Treasury, distributed by the University Grants Committee (UGC), a quango with a mix of professional members, supported by a Treasury civil servant. All other forms of national public education and training post-15 were not a central government responsibility, but were run by local authorities, technical and craft organizations awarding certificates (City and Guilds, for example), evening courses providing administrative, technical, and secretarial skills, teacher and clerical training colleges, or other independent bodies.

From the early twentieth century, if a large town or city thought that it had the resources and the ambition to found a "university", it could develop academic programmes locally, and gradually establish ones of "degree level", but it could not award its own degrees. Southampton was a case in point in establishing Hartley University College in 1902 (previously Hartley Institution since 1862), which secured many civic supporters, among whom was Milner's father as its treasurer before 1914, also representing an extension arm of the University of Cambridge. After 1918, a new device was widely adopted to enable these local educational colleges to become "university" colleges with degree-recognized powers that were validated by a neighbouring fully constituted university. The University College in Newcastle, for example, provided degree-level courses, but they were validated by the University of Durham, so that the candidate formally became a Durham graduate.

---

[16] York Civic Trust Annual Reports 1946–50, YML.

In 1947, the post-war Labour government had no clear plan for post-18 education or training. The Percy and Barlow reports were attempts to clarify what such a policy might be. Their publication encouraged a flurry of interest around the country and some two dozen civic declarations of interest were submitted to the UGC, of which York's was one. Its delegation attending the UGC included Morrell, Sheldon, and Milner. But it was a premature move in most cases. The minutes of the UGC make it very clear that it was not anticipating an immediate increase in the numbers of suitably qualified 18-year-olds wishing to attend university, and, even if there was, the existing capacity, especially within the "university" colleges, was sufficient.[17] Furthermore, what sort of increase might it be? If it was largely to be in science and engineering, as was widely favoured, where should such new universities be located? From this perspective, York was not an obvious choice, something also true for other applicants. This message was conveyed to the York delegation, with the suggestion that they should build on what existing facilities and resources could be developed to support higher education and training. In the unlikely scenario that the government wished to establish wholly new universities, the city would then be in a better position to apply.

Many of the towns and cities bidding for a "new" university in 1947 were again bidding in the very different environment in 1958. They probably had all received the same earlier advice from Sir Walter Moberly (1881–1974, chairman of the UGC 1935–49), while acting upon it in different ways.[18] In the case of York, the core group of individual enthusiasts continued to come from the Civic Trust, along with some support from the city's Director of Education and individual councillors, usually those also active in the Civic Trust. It had established an academic subcommittee in 1947, and asked Milner to chair it, which he did until success was achieved in 1960 with the UGC's decision that Norwich and York were to be the first locations selected. Milner and J. B. Morrell

---

[17]   For the University Grants Committee's discussions about student numbers, 1950–6, Warren, *Eric James*, p. 141, fn 12.

[18]   Sir Walter Hamilton Moberly (1881–1974), *ODNB*, vol. 38, pp. 477–8.

remained the two most consistently supportive individuals in the city throughout the decade following Sheldon's early death in 1951.

But it is important not to over-inflate Milner's role in this period. As the second citizen, he was an enthusiastic promoter, with an adaptable and flexible vision for his adopted home city. But he was principally a priest, presiding over one of the most significant cathedrals in the country and a leading cleric in the Church of England. In coming into office in 1951, the Conservative government saw no immediate reason to change policy towards the university system over the next six years. Nevertheless, throughout that period, Milner gave considerable thought to alternatives in relation to what might be possible in York. For instance, might a single donor be found to fund a post-graduate college, as Oxford had done in the figure of Lord Nuffield, but with a focus on the arts, "an All Souls of the North"? Alternatively, might York create a "College for Britain" to reflect rising interest in British history and culture around the English-speaking world, particularly among the Dominions and the developing Commonwealth? Or again, should York encourage a constellation of post-graduate professional training courses in areas in which York was rich in resources—the choice decided upon initially?

As we have seen, Milner's talents and personality were never seen as those of a potential diocesan bishop. One of Milner's traits, however, was to choose colleagues usually with the right talents and sharing his own ideals and approach. These were often young men from Oxford or Cambridge (ideally from King's), who would be given their head. Even in the case of the restoration of the Minster's glass, upon which Milner did want to be totally in charge, he nevertheless allowed and encouraged the young apprentice, Peter Gibson, to emerge as the main worker on the glass.[19]

It was this trait that led Milner to make his most significant contribution to the Civic Trust to locate a "new university at York" in 1960. This was the appointment of John West-Taylor, as the paid secretary of the Trust's

---

[19]   Peter Gibson (1929–2016): Superintendent, The York Glaziers Trust, see Wikipedia entry. Also, Peter Gibson, "A Treasure House of Stained Glass", in Holtby, *Milner-White: A Memorial*, pp. 59–81.

academic subcommittee in the afterglow of the success of York's Festival of Britain, later in 1951.

John West-Taylor (1924–91) had been educated at St George's School, Windsor and at Cranleigh, where the young J. S. Purvis, important much later in York, was a history teacher and assistant chaplain. West-Taylor had been accepted by Trinity Hall, Cambridge to read music and history, which was subsequently delayed by war service in the RAF.[20] A cultivated young man, interested in music, art, architecture, and archives, he lodged in Cambridge at the home of Henry Morris, Chief Education Officer for Cambridgeshire. Morris, as we have seen, had been appointed at an unexpectedly early age, after graduating in 1920 as a slightly mature student from King's College. In a poor county educationally, he had pioneered village community colleges, which had won him an international reputation. He believed that the county's schools should have stylish, modern community buildings set in expansive grounds, with fine artwork on the walls. Pre-war examples included Impington, Sawston and Linton. He attracted undergraduates interested in art and architecture, some of whom lodged with him as John did, also acting as his chauffeur. Among other earlier examples was Harry Ree, later a war hero in the Special Operations Executive, headmaster and founding professor of education at the University of York. Milner may well have known Morris as a King's undergraduate in 1920, reading philosophy, but not now intending to be ordained. While in no sense a typical "King's" man, Milner in the 1930s was describing Morris as a "friend".[21]

With these qualities and connections, it was no surprise that Milner selected John West-Taylor for the job of secretary of the academic committee of the Civic Trust in 1951. His responsibilities were to build upon the early initiatives of the Civic Trust in response to the UGC's feedback in 1947.

The first of these was the idea that York should develop a provision for advanced professional architectural training and practice for historic

20   Warren, *Eric James*, pp. 18–19.
21   Milner-White to Alfred Wayment, nd. 1939, KCAC/Modern Archives/ EMW/X/2/Wayment/1.

buildings, as well as for local authorities in building the new secondary schools, following the 1944 Education Act.

The second was the need to find a solution, especially in cathedral towns and in rural counties, to the problems of conservation and public access to their historic civic and ecclesiastical records. In some cathedral towns, this was seen as potentially a collaboration between the cathedral and the diocese through the dean and chapter and the diocesan registrar. At first, this had seemed the best way forward in the case of York, but these discussions had been abruptly terminated in 1949 by Milner personally. A new solution was needed. Ironically, Milner's action led to a better and simpler solution than the earlier scheme, involving just two main parties—the city council, that had to find a new use for the medieval St Anthony's Hall on Peaseholme Green, and the diocese of York, with the Minster and its dean and chapter taking a supportive role.[22] Aided by an unexpected legacy, funding was found from the estate of William Borthwick from Bridlington, home town of Canon Purvis.

As a result, two new foundation stones could be laid, in response to the UGC's advice in 1947 about a possible future university for the city. Both involved the reuse of historic assets in the city for contemporary use—the King's Manor and St Anthony's Hall. Milner was closely involved, not so much as Dean of York, but more as joint secretary of the York Civic Trust and chairman of its academic subcommittee, a difference often not understood by York's citizens, quite understandably.

For John West-Taylor and his wife, Catherine, his appointment as the salaried arm of the academic subcommittee was the beginning of a 40-year journey of initiatives, campaigns, applications, frustrations, and successes, all ultimately leading to the opening of the university in October 1963, with John West-Taylor as the founding registrar (1961–89). A discreet, talented, and creative man, he was a perfect foil for his two very different bosses, Dean Milner-White and Lord James of Rusholme as the founding vice-chancellor.

In 1951, Milner was 67 and John West-Taylor over 30 years younger, so what little we know of their personal dynamic is speculative. John's widow

---

[22] Borthwick Institute for Archives, see <https://www.york.ac.uk/borthwick/abouttheborthwick/history/>, accessed 3 October 2024.

commented many years later to the author that her late husband did not fully trust Milner, such was his mode of operation, something explicitly alluded to in the Wilkinson memoir and by others. Nevertheless, Milner had already been Dean of York for ten years and was to be so for another twelve, and had developed an influential and discreet presence in the city's life, as well as his specific role within the Minster and the wider Church of England.

Regarding the prospects of a full university being created in the city, the initial years were only modestly successful as far as Milner and his academic subcommittee were concerned. The appointment of John West-Taylor as executive secretary allowed the development of an Institute for Advanced Architectural Studies and the Borthwick Institute of Historical Research to be realized, and a programme of summer schools was launched. Milner oversaw these initiatives, continuing to float imaginative possibilities but without any real prospect of success. No single benefactor appeared and a College for Britain remained a pipedream. He was able to have a high-profile opening of the Borthwick Institute by the Princess Royal, with an address from Sir Maurice Bowra, President of the British Academy. More fundamentally, the attitude of the University Grants Committee and its Treasury masters remained as it had been in 1947, that any expansion of undergraduate student numbers could be absorbed by existing institutions with only two very particular exceptions.[23]

By 1958, Milner was pessimistic about prospects for any future university at York.[24]

But within a few weeks, John West-Taylor was reporting that there seemed to be a change of the "mood music" within the centre of government, both among ministers and senior Treasury civil servants, about the founding of "new" universities, probably two in the first instance.

---

[23]   Warren, *Eric James*, pp. 14–17. The exceptions were Keele and Sussex. See the case studies on the Universities of Keele (1957), Sussex (1960), and York (1963) by Miles Taylor, Matthew Cragoe, and Allen Warren respectively in Jill Pellew and Miles Taylor (eds), *Utopian Universities: A Global History of the New Campuses of the 1960s* (London: Bloomsbury, 2021).

[24]   Warren, *Eric James*, p. 16, fn. 15.

This development is almost certainly one of delayed consequences of the major governmental battle over financial and economic policy, which had resulted in early 1958 in the collective resignation of the whole ministerial Treasury team of Peter Thorneycroft, Enoch Powell, and Nigel Birch; "a little local difficulty" in Harold Macmillan's famous phrase. In very broad terms, the ministers were "monetarists" and the Treasury civil servants "Keynesians"—the Prime Minister sided with the Keynesians in a policy of economic expansion rather than financial restraint in the run-up to a general election, anticipated in 1959. The timescale would be tight if there were to be political benefits at the election. The commitment to fund wholly "new" universities as an element within the overall change of Treasury policy was relatively easy in governmental terms, as universities were directly funded by the Treasury.

John West-Taylor was very clear that York's case would have to be prepared speedily. Milner was fully supportive but had little knowledge of the university world beyond King's College, Cambridge. John did all the preparatory work during 1959 for eventual submission to the UGC. What Milner could supply was his ability to influence personally the context of how a decision might be arrived at. In this case, the overall lead was taken by Archbishop Michael Ramsey, whom Milner had known since the 1920s—both as an academic and archbishop. An invitation was extended to Sir Keith Murray, a distinguished agricultural scientist from Oxford, and now an experienced and powerful chairman of the UGC, to visit York, staying at the Deanery overnight. The following morning, Murray was taken by John West-Taylor and Milner to view the potential site at Heslington from the nearby water tower, with its panoramic view over the whole site, centred around Heslington Hall. It made a deep impression on Murray, who commented on what he saw as a wonderful environment for a university: "The lawns and trees give a very gracious setting—a very important factor."[25]

This was followed by a meeting with York's representatives at Bishopthorpe Palace, under the eye of Michael Ramsey. Encouraged by these conversations, plans to make a submission later in the year advanced

---

[25]   Keith Anderson Hope Murray, Baron Murray of Newhaven (1903–93): *ODNB*, vol. 39, pp. 967–8; Warren, *Eric James*, p. 18.

rapidly between Milner, John West-Taylor and the civic authorities, with the Lord Mayor hosting public meetings at the Mansion House. The resulting document written by John putting the York case to the UGC was later described by Murray as a "masterpiece". It was considered along with that of Norwich the following April 1960 and accepted. The long ambition to create a full university for the city had been won. Milner had contributed little directly to that bidding document as far as is known, but it is reasonable to assume that he supported the tentative suggestion that the university's overall structure might include a college system for the twentieth century.[26]

With this national endorsement, planning took on a different tempo and Milner's involvement reduced, with continuity being sustained by the clear assumption that John West-Taylor would be appointed as founding registrar. Milner, increasingly unwell, was kept appraised of developments, including the architectural practice appointed, Robert Matthew/Johnson-Marshall, themselves well known to West-Taylor as friends and collaborators of Henry Morris (Milner's earlier Cambridge friend).

It seems very likely that Stirratt Johnson-Marshall was the person suggesting that drainage problems on the proposed Heslington site might be solved by the creation of a central artificial lake, on which Milner is said to have commented that it would be something like the Backs in Cambridge. Rather surprisingly, given his role at the time as chairman of the Diocesan Advisory Committee and his other academic interests, Milner is not known to have intervened significantly. John West-Taylor was the critical element in the initial development of the site, with the founding vice-chancellor, Lord James, admitting that he did not know much about architecture at this time.

Nor did Milner campaign for a chapel or a chaplaincy on the campus, accepting that the university should be a secular institution, although at his death he was planning a founding service in the Minster; his last special service in October 1963. It was acknowledged that Heslington parish church would serve the spiritual needs of Anglican students and staff. What was agreed was that the dean and chapter would gift a green

---

26   Warren, *Eric James*, pp. 18–29.

space between Heslington Hall and the church to the university, thereby supporting the aesthetic of the place.[27]

---

[27]   Warren, *Eric James*, pp. 29–31.

The Minster and the Dean, 1941–63

As regards the daily work and worship of the Minster itself, there was not much scope in 1941 for innovation, with much of the glass removed for safekeeping, as well as the constraints of food, material, and fuel controls, in addition to the blackout.

Addresses to the chapter and the Friends of York Minster gave some hint of Milner's priorities in "beautifying" the Minster, often through gifts of artefacts, textiles, and ecclesiastical vestments. Lady Milner-White paid for new choir stalls for the nave. This was to be combined with the conduct of its regular liturgy including music and movement, using the potential of the whole building as well as its more private spaces, and in ways not previously available to him at King's. He also rather surprisingly suggested, as an aspiration, the construction of a cloister at the north-eastern end of the Minster, an idea only returned to in the late 1950s, and in a very different context.[1] As to the regular liturgy, he wished to build upon the restrained and dignified traditions of the Caroline Divines, "catholic but English", in Percy Dearmer's phrase.[2] As the Minster was sometimes regarded as the "highest" in England, there was no need for more incense, as Canon Bell had hinted in his letter to Lang in 1941. During the remaining years of the war, there were also limited opportunities, especially within choral and sacred music, given that the Minster organist and master of the choristers was Sir Edward Bairstow, who had held the position since 1913, had been knighted in 1932 for

---

[1]   YML, Milner's Address to the Full Chapter, 13 January 1942, York Minster Archives—Minutes of Full Chapter, Friends of York Minster, Annual Report 1942.

[2]   Percy Dearmer (1867–1936), *ODNB*, vol. 15, pp. 652–3.

his services to church music and was a doughty West Yorkshireman.[3] In addition, any special services were a challenge—exceptions being the service of dedication of a chapel in the Minster to the West Yorkshire Regiment in 1942 and a number of services in 1943 dedicated to youth organizations.[4]

In May 1945, with the end of hostilities in Europe, Milner had been dean for over three years—a surprising choice in what was becoming increasingly a global conflict. Milner's response to this new situation had enabled him to fashion a role for himself as the presumptive first post-war Dean of York, fully integrated into the civic life of the city. At the same time, he could now personally redirect the way in which one of the great cathedrals of Europe could fulfil its key Christian purposes, as well as having a broader impact on the spiritual life of the nation. It comes as no surprise therefore that these themes remain almost inseparable over the remaining years of his life. Disentangling them for present purposes is almost inevitably rather mechanistic, for which the author apologizes.

After the war, a more normal pattern of services could resume, although materials, labour and fundraising were still highly restricted. Sunday worship retained its centrepiece—choral Matins and sermon, followed by choral communion—despite his views on Matins as expressed to the Fellows of King's in 1918.

Special services at the Minster had not been common before 1939, except those traditionally associated with the armed services, the judicial year, or the Northern Province. But, following the National Day of Prayer in May 1940 and others during the war, Milner was able to give greater attention to this dimension of cathedral worship more civically and thematically. Just two examples, both national and local, in the Battle of Britain Sunday Service from the early 1950s, and in Milner's agreement that the York Boy Scouts' annual rededication to their promise and laws could be held in the Minster on a Sunday adjacent to St George's Day (23 April), followed by a parade through the city. This paralleled the annual national service of King's Scouts since 1935 in St George's Chapel, Windsor, normally preceded by a review by the King (as patron) or other

---

3   Sir Edward Cuthbert Bairstow (1874–1946), *ODNB*, vol. 3, p. 354.

4   YML, Service Orders 1943 to 1947.

leading members of the Royal Family. Both were good precedents. By the early 1950s, at York, there was a regular programme of such special services.[5]

But two occasions prompted services, which gave Milner scope to plan and choreograph events of national significance, but within a Yorkshire context. Both also played to a widely and popularly expressed cultural and civic notion that the city of York was the historic "capital" of Yorkshire.

The first, in June 1951, was at the beginning of the city's own Festival of Britain at a service in the Minster, attended by the King's sister, the Princess Royal, Countess of Harewood, along with the Prime Minister and Mrs Attlee, and all the mayors of Yorkshire. Following this explicitly Yorkshire opening, a civic reception was hosted by the Lord Mayor at the Mansion House. At its conclusion, guests moved outdoors to the Museum Gardens and the ruins of St Mary's Abbey for the first performance since 1580 of a sequence of the city's Mystery Plays, a centrepiece of the festival, in a new edition prepared by the scholarly Canon J. S. Purvis of the Minster and priest of St Olave's, Marygate. It was also possibly the first appearance on a public stage of (Dame) Judi Dench, then a school pupil of York. Unlike the national festival, which was primarily linked to science, architecture, modern technology and manufacture, York City Council had successfully bid as one of the endorsed provincial centres for festivals with a theme of the arts and heritage. Two sacred concerts

---

[5]   For example, YML, Service Orders, 1955 (10th Anniversary of the ending of the Second World War)—23 January 1955 Epiphany Service with Carols; 1 May 1955 Service of Thanksgiving for Victory in War; 7 May 1955 Service of Pilgrimage of Sunday Schools from the East Riding; 28 June 1955 St Peter's Evensong and the presentation of Women's Offering; 1 August 1955 King's Own Yorkshire Light Infantry Service for the Regiment's 200th Anniversary and the Laying Up of Colours, in the presence of Queen Elizabeth, the Queen Mother, the Colonel in Chief; 18 September 1955 Service for Victory in the Battle of Britain; 2 October 1955 Harvest Thanksgiving; 22 October 1955 Service for the Central Councils of the YMCA and the YWCA; 1 November 1955 Service for the RAF fallen, in the presence of the Duke of Edinburgh; 24 November 1955 Festival of Nine Lessons and Carols.

were held in the Minster during the festival—Elgar's *The Dream of Gerontius*, with Sir John Barbirolli conducting, and soloists Heddle Nash and Gladys Ripley (replacing Kathleen Ferrier, who was unwell), and Verdi's *Requiem* with da Sabata conducting and Elisabeth Schwarzkopf as soprano soloist. Across the city, a two-week-long programme of popular music, theatre and exhibitions was staged, along with features on the future of public housing for the post-war world, while the national Camping and Caravanning Club held its annual gathering within the city. It also allowed the reopened City Art Gallery to highlight its own collections as well as those of individual Yorkshire families, and for the wider public to see the changes brought about by its new curator, Hans Hess. Unlike the festival on the South Bank that had its right-wing critics as an expensive socialist stunt dreamt up by Herbert Morrison, the York Festival was politically uncontroversial and a popular success. In the celebratory speeches at the end of the festival, in the presence of national representatives, the call for York to have a university was made again.[6]

As so often in Milner's life, an opportunity had arisen, not of his own creation, but which provided him with the chance to give an idea "vision" and momentum, along with a distinctive form and content so that it could become more than its originators had aspired to.

This was also true in my second example in 1961, when the present Duke of Kent married Katharine Worsley in the first royal wedding in York Minster since 1328, attended by the whole Royal Family and many other European royal representatives. It was also possibly the first occasion that an official royal occasion outside London was screened on television, as well as receiving major coverage in cinemas on Pathe News. Conducted by Archbishop Ramsey, about to move to Canterbury, it put the city and its Minster on the map, along with all things Yorkshire. Once again, it showed Milner's capacity to exploit an opportunity to realize his ambition for cathedrals and larger Anglican churches to play a more significant role in the public worship of England: one of the identifying features of his interpretation of the national religious story. It also allowed "God's own county" to reinforce its own self-image. The

---

6   For extensive Yorkshire press coverage, BNA, 1 to 20 June 1951, especially *The Yorkshire Post and Leeds Intelligencer*, and the *Bradford Observer*.

local and northern press had a field day: "Yorkshire lass/squire's daughter marries Royal Duke", etc. It no doubt helped that the bride's father, Sir William Worsley of Hovingham Hall, near Helmsley, came from a landed family, which had a long tradition of public service within Yorkshire. In 1961, he was Lord Lieutenant of the North Riding. More importantly for many was the fact that he had played for and captained Yorkshire County Cricket Club in the late 1920s and was now its president, something which cricket-loving Milner would have appreciated.[7]

Cathedrals as homes for all the arts

In 1952, Milner was invited by his old pupil from before 1914, Seiriol Evans, about to become the Dean of Gloucester, to address the Friends of the Cathedral on his chosen theme of "Cathedral: Home of All the Arts". On his own arrival at York in 1941, Milner had on more than one occasion identified the "beautifying" of the Minster as one of his major ambitions, a theme identified by Peter Young in his unpublished paper at the Milner-White seminar in 2016. Given the range of Milner's own aesthetic and artistic interests—church glass, Japanese stoneware, the classical ballet, fabrics, and furniture, wrought ironwork, and fine book printing, binding, and illustration—it is tempting to separate out these enthusiasms individually, without considering features they may have had in common in defining his aestheticism. Anecdotally at least, he is recorded as greeting a new diocesan appointment for the first time in 1960 at the Deanery with the words: "I gather that you are interested in beautiful things."[8]

It makes the point that Milner's historical training and perspective is very different from that of today. This needs to be understood particularly in relation to some of his more controversial decisions as dean, especially

---

[7]   There was extensive radio, television and press coverage throughout the British Isles as well as on Pathe News, with a focus not only on the royal dimension, but also on the event as a Yorkshire occasion, with the white rose featuring prominently on the hats and dresses of the royal party.

[8]   Private information.

in relation to his approach to the reinstallation and restoration of the Minster's medieval glass from 1948. In this sphere, it is interesting to "compare and contrast" the career, attitudes, and interests of a younger eminent man of the arts—Kenneth Clark. A reading of his entry in the *Oxford Dictionary of National Biography* is instructive.

1 2

The city of York, the Minster glass, the Pilgrim Trust, and the Dean

Introduction

In previous chapters, we have seen how Milner rapidly integrated himself into the life of the city elites and their collective post-war vision as expressed in J. B. Morrell's *York: City of Our Dreams* in 1940. As he became a more significant civic figure from 1942 onwards, it became obvious that the Minster, iconically at least, would be part of that vision, once the Dean and Chapter had decided in late 1944 that its greatest post-war priority would be the reinstallation and restoration of its medieval glass.

They also recognized that this would be a considerable challenge, financially, practically, aesthetically and in the world of scholarship. It was a project of nearly 20 years, only coming to its completion at the time of Milner's death in June 1963.[1]

This proved subsequently to be the most controversial aspect of Milner's tenure as Dean of York, at least within the academic community

---

[1] The archival material on this particular history is extensive, but the bulk is to be found in York Minster Library, in the Milner-White papers and his annual reports to the Friends of York Minster, and in the London Metropolitan Archives, City of London Corporation, 40 Northampton Road, London, EC1R 0HB in the Pilgrim Trust Archive, especially in the Short History of the Trust (LMA/4450), the Trust Minutes 1945 to 1951 (LMA/4450/A/01/012–016), and in the Secretary's Papers (LMA/4450/A/03/1945 to 1951).

of art historians of medieval glass, with their evolving opinions on the principles of good practice in conservation, cleaning, and restoration.

During his lifetime, Milner had a reputation as the leading scholar and practitioner in the world of ecclesiastical glass, with it being a significant element contributing to his award of the CBE in 1952, and his honorary Doctorate of Letters by the University of Leeds in 1962. But the decade and a half following his death saw significant changes in the scholarly world of art history and in the study of stained glass, which introduced a dissenting opinion. In 1977, an authoritative history of York Minster by a group of independent scholars was published by Oxford University Press, edited by G. E. Aylmer (head of the newly founded History Department at York) and Canon R. E. Cant (Canon Chancellor of the Minster). In the essay on the Minster's medieval glass, two young art historians, David O'Connor and Jeremy Haselock, took issue with Milner's reputation in respect of the restoration and rearrangement of the glass in the chapter house and in the Great East Window. The international significance particularly of the two windows, and the status of the volume gave their essay a continuing importance, influencing Milner's posthumous reputation.

The present author is not competent to judge these contrasting scholarly opinions, in which Professor Brown substantially endorses the critical elements in the O'Connor and Haselock essay of 1977. She adds, however, that in taking the restoration project "as a whole", Milner's contribution was "heroic".[2]

The following account by a twentieth-century British historian attempts to place that "heroic" achievement in its context of Britain in the years after 1945.

Since his death, Milner's personality and his scholarly reputation has divided both academic opinion and those more generally informed about internationally significant "heritage" sites. Given that Milner was

---

[2]   Sarah Brown, *Stained Glass at York Minster*, 2017, especially pp. 29–30, 97–8, 100–1. For the best summary of Professor Brown's views, see the proceedings of the 2016 Milner-White seminar, which she has most generously allowed me to paraphrase (in my words), pending her own plans to write fully on this subject.

not someone who paraded his abilities in terms of research, this has reinforced these divisions, as it has in other areas of his life. Nevertheless, there is enough published evidence of that time on how he addressed the very specific problems in relation to medieval church glass in situ. For this writer, not an expert, the best evidence can be found in Milner's contributions to *The Burlington Magazine*, at that time probably the most significant academic art history journal in English, particularly his article entitled "The Resurrection of a 14th century window" (1952) and his review of Christopher Woodforde's *English Stained and Painted Glass* (1954). The first is an account of rediscovering and reconstructing a single early fourteenth-century window in the Minster, the second a review of Christopher Woodforde's attempt to condense his knowledge and understanding of stained glass in a short, single volume for a more general readership.[3] In each of these different academic contributions, the reader sees Milner's forensic and intuitive methodology, as the reader does in his more practical and reflective other writings about stained glass in the decade. In the case of the Woodforde volume, there is a more than generous appreciation of the author's achievement in successfully compressing a highly complex subject within a short and accessible compass.[4] In both these *Burlington* pieces, a frivolous reader might see why Milner would have such a passion for detective fiction. Milner saw painting on glass as a "mosaic" art and its study a combination of hard evidence, probability, and imaginative intuition, not unrelated to the talents of Sherlock Holmes.

---

[3]   The Revd Christopher Woodforde (1907–62), Fellow and Chaplain, New College, Oxford 1948–59.

[4]   Eric Milner-White, "The Resurrection of a late 14th century window, apprenticeship, stained glass", *Burlington Magazine* 94:589 (1952), pp. 108–12. For Milner's review of Christopher Woodforde, *English Stained and Painted Glass* (Oxford: Clarendon Press, 1954), see *Burlington Magazine* 97:629 (1955), pp. 262–3.

The Pilgrim Trust

Turning away from these important, scholarly concerns, what was to be critical in any discussion of the post-war development and conservation of York is the part played by the Pilgrim Trust across the city. This included not only the Minster, but also other city churches, the Merchant Taylors' and the Merchant Adventurers' Halls, the Borthwick Institute of Historical Research, the York Glaziers Trust, the York Council for Conservation, and the planning of the new University of York. That comprehensive engagement in the post-war reconstruction of the city, often co-ordinated by the Civic Trust, has not been sufficiently recognized within the city. At the centre of almost all these projects is the figure of Milner-White, with, at times, his controversial and unilateral decisions on the Minster's behalf. As a result, today's popular image of him among those informed and interested in the Minster has become distorted. In part, this is because of the sheer numbers of projects in which he was involved, but more significantly because the archives of the Pilgrim Trust have hardly been consulted, if at all. Most researchers have understandably focussed on records located in York, rather than those of the Pilgrim Trust, lodged in the City of London Metropolitan Archive, along with those of its secretary, Lord Kilmaine. By consulting the Trust's formal minutes, policy discussions and decisions, as well as the papers of its secretary, a very much more comprehensive picture emerges, involving issues for the Church of England principally in respect of its historic inheritance, preservation, and conservation, alongside its fundamental Christian purpose. All of this had to be conducted in the atmosphere of austerity in post-war Britain. Among many elements in play was whether central government had a role (hardly a priority), within which the procrastination of the Church of England, especially that of Geoffrey Fisher, was not helpful. The issue was only resolved finally through a motion at the meeting of the Church Assembly in 1951, orchestrated by politician and campaigner Ivor Bulmer-Thomas. The resulting committee, chaired by Bulmer-Thomas, who also wrote its report, led the institutional Church to accept overall responsibility for its cathedrals and parish churches along with associated policies. Kilmaine, Milner and the Pilgrim Trust were all critically involved in that challenging debate and its resolution through a refashioned Central Council for Church Conservation, to be chaired by Milner's former pupil and friend, Dean Seiriol Evans of Gloucester. Milner was almost inevitably a prominent member.[5]

Another surprisingly under-consulted source for Milner's views on church glass are the minutes and associated papers of the York Diocesan Advisory Committee, which he chaired from 1944 until his death. Through its diocesan role in the granting of faculties, his committee had an important impact on about thirty parish churches who wished to enhance their church through newly commissioned windows, additional "furniture and fittings", and reordered spaces.[6]

Returning, however, to the challenges facing the dean and chapter from 1945 onwards.

Firstly, how was the ambition to reinstate and restore the Minster's glass (some 80 windows) to be realized during the long period of immediate post-war public austerity and extensive central government regulation, and in which the restoration of non-war-damaged churches was not a priority? Secondly, how relevant was the fact that the Church of England had no corporate strategy for its churches and cathedrals, other than at the highly local or diocesan level? Thirdly, what was the overall public and governmental mood on these questions of restoration, rather than the enthusiasm for the relatively few iconic examples of re-creation as triumphantly realized in Coventry Cathedral? Fourthly, to what degree were aspects of Milner's personality, along with his own more panoramic views on the role of stained glass in relation to worship, at variance with changing orthodoxies of art historians and preservationists? What follows is the author's exercise in walking on eggshells.

As Henry Hinchcliffe has remarked, Milner was largely self-taught in relation to the arts in almost all its forms, not at all untypical of his very English education at Harrow and King's before 1914. His tutor, Oscar Browning, was representative of a mentality already coming

---

[5]   Ivor Bulmer-Thomas (1905–93): *ODNB*, vol. 58, p. 334.

[6]   Faculty—in ecclesiastical law, the dispensation or licence for diocesan permission to alter the church fabric, church yards and the curtilage and significant furnishings of a parish church. *ODCC*, pp. 564–5.

under modest challenge in Oxford and Cambridge by the Edwardian period. Milner seems to have been motivated, as were many others, by tours during the vacations of historic European cathedrals, often with his friend, Philip Loyd, the detail of which he retained very precisely.[7] In becoming responsible for King's College Chapel in 1918 with an already formed aesthetic and sacramental churchmanship, Milner was suddenly responsible for one of the most renowned late medieval buildings in northern Europe, but supported in the case of its glass by the definitive scholarship of the Provost, M. R. James, and within a corporate environment very different from his later position as Dean of York. As a result, we only get hints in the interwar years about his general opinions and approach, through the windows installed in the Memorial Chapel at King's, one of which was dedicated to his closest friend at Harrow and King's, Captain Gerald Fitzgerald. Later we see evidence in the new church at Bitterne, his parental home, built in large part in memory of his father, and, finally, in the window in York Minster in memory of Bishop Philip Loyd, his closest friend among the Trappists, in 1952. Milner personally paid significantly in each case. A very different perspective can also be seen in his report on the stained glass in Ely Cathedral, presented to the Friends of the Cathedral in 1937, shortly after Milner had joined the Ely Diocesan Advisory Committee. In these examples, Milner is concerned either with "new" windows or commenting on the extensive early Victorian transformation of a cathedral's glass.[8]

Nevertheless, we get an insight into Milner's aesthetic, spiritual, and historical perspective. In the case of the Fitzgerald memorial and the much later memorial window to Philip Loyd in York Minster, we see the ambition to tell a personal story through the purchase and presentation of existing glass and fashioning it to cast "light" on the individual memorialized—in Fitzgerald's case with glass from his home area in Essex, and in Loyd's with high-quality Flemish glass that had been used in the church in Rickmansworth, subsequently removed in the Victorian period, but retained in store. Milner personally purchased this glass, locating the Essex glass so that the sun would focus light at certain times

7   Wilkinson, *Milner-White*, p. 10.

8   Montague Rhodes, James (1862–1936), *ODNB*, vol. 29, p. 723.

on Fitzgerald's name, and the Rickmansworth glass to remind the viewer that Loyd had been Bishop of St Albans, the diocese in which the parish is situated. At Bitterne, the church was closely supervised by Milner and his mother, with the glass being a mixture of familiar sacred themes and a civic tableau reflecting Southampton's maritime history as well as one of its most famous citizens, the poet and hymnodist Isaac Watts. In the case of Ely, Milner saw his remit differently. He produced a bluntly critical report of the way the Victorian deans and their chapters had approached the most significant addition to the cathedral's glass, both in terms of its quality and conception. Much of it could be simply removed in Milner's opinion, with him concluding that retention of some panels might be justified on "historic rather than artistic grounds". Interestingly, 15 years later Pevsner gave his own characterful judgement:

> But as to the Victorian glass, Ely is a mine inexhaustible to those
> of somewhat morbid curiosity, who wish to study it. As the names
> of the artists are recorded with unusual care, a list follows here
> without much comment.[9]

These relatively minor episodes have been introduced at this point to underline how Milner's priorities in relation to ecclesiastical glass, both

---

[9]   On the glass of King's College, Cambridge, M. R. James, with an appendix by Eric Milner-White, *A Guide to the Windows of King's College, Cambridge* (Cambridge: Cambridge University Press, 1930). On the Church of the Ascension, Bitterne, Southampton, Nikolaus Pevsner and David Lloyd, *The Buildings of England: Hampshire and the Isle of Wight* (London: Penguin Books, 1967), pp. 590–2. Also, YML, Yorkshire Special Collections 59-2-23— File of Texts and Photographs prepared at about the time of construction. On Ely Cathedral, Nikolaus Pevsner, *The Buildings of England: Cambridgeshire and the Isle of Ely* (London: Penguin Books, 1954), pp. 288–90. Milner-White 1937 Report on the Windows of Ely Cathedral, for first annual Report of the Friends of the Cathedral, YML, RR Pamphlets, Box 65/25.

new and restored, were not those of today's scholarly art historians or heritage professionals.[10]

In 1940, the medieval glass had been removed largely at the Minster's own expense. There were few reserves for its restoration and reinstallation. So, how was it to be paid for?

The Church of England was, of course, a very wealthy institution, as were the Oxbridge colleges and the London livery companies, but its assets were very unevenly spread between the Church Commissioners (established in 1836) and the dioceses, cathedrals, and individual parishes more widely. In addition, its structures of overall church governance were weak, with great autonomy given to the diocesan bishop or the individual dean. Each was expected to live "off their own", with the Commissioners taking restricted responsibilities according to statute or ecclesiastical law. In addition, central and local government had very little power to interfere, feeling almost no responsibility towards functioning buildings as distinct from ruins or abandoned sites (through the Ministry of Works). In an environment in which many urban churches had been destroyed or severely damaged by enemy action, renewal, including churches, was a new problem in a context in which government was to all intents bankrupt. At the same time, national and local government needed to refashion industry, social infrastructure, education, health, and welfare as well as rebuild or construct modern domestic housing. It is no surprise therefore that the Church of England turned to external sources for help, in this case the Pilgrim Trust, with applications quickly exceeding funding available. Who was going to succeed in this scramble for resources was not obvious.

It is probably true to say that the Pilgrim Trust was the most significant body in the UK in the preservation of historical buildings, both ecclesiastical and secular, from the 1930s until the 1960s.[11] Founded on the enormous benefaction of American Edward Harkness in 1930, and its judicious investment, it could fund, along with its Harkness Scholarship

---

[10] For Milner's substantial impact on glass restoration in parish churches in the diocese of York as chairman of the Diocesan Advisory Committee from 1944 until his death, see below pp. 138–53.

[11] <https://www.thepilgrimtrust.org.uk/>, accessed 3 October 2024.

scheme, conservation, preservation and community programmes to the tune of £400,000 annually by 1945, of which just under one third was devoted to ecclesiastical projects.[12] The city of York was probably its most significant beneficiary, the Minster above all, enabling it to reinstall, preserve, and restore its unique medieval glass. At some not recorded point, the Pilgrim Trust had agreed that the city of York would be one of its largest projects in the ten years after 1945. For his part, Cyril Garbett as Archbishop of York had already secured Pilgrim Trust support to restore some of the city's parish churches in 1944, and some English dioceses were making plans to try and integrate their registries and archives, often in partnership with their own cathedral/minster, of which York was one. Whether consciously or not, this proved to be a fortunate convergence of aspirations for the Minster, the York Civic Trust, and the English legacy of Edward Harkness.

The Pilgrim Trustees themselves were a very grand group including Stanley Baldwin, as the original chairman, Tom Jones (a former Cabinet Secretary) as secretary, and John Buchan, with Lord Macmillan (1873–1952), one of the most distinguished lawyers of his generation, as chairman since 1935. It had appointed a new secretary in late 1944, the Hon. John Browne, who inherited his family title of Lord Kilmaine the following year. An Irish peer and an experienced public servant and building conservationist, he and Milner may have already known each other. Browne had been secretary of University College, Southampton (de facto registrar) from 1929 to 1933. Earlier, Hartley College (its precursor) had been greatly supported by Milner's father, Sir Henry Milner-White, as treasurer, benefactor, and representative of the University of Cambridge on its board. Milner's mother may have continued to live in Bitterne after his death in 1922, and both she and Milner were closely involved in the building and decoration of the new church. Although always using the conventions of the time in formal communications, it is highly unlikely that Milner and Kilmaine were totally unaware of one another in 1945.[13]

---

[12] LMA/Pilgrim Trust Minutes, 1944—Report on Distribution of Funds 1930–44.

[13] John Browne, 6th Baron Kilmaine (1902–78).

The dean and chapter in York were not the first "off the blocks" in the city—bids for support had already been submitted by the York Philosophical Society in respect of St John's Micklegate, by the Merchant Taylors of York in relation to their fifteenth-century hall, and by Archbishop Garbett in the case of the city centre parish churches. As in other cathedral towns, plans were being made in relation to diocesan archives and registries in collaboration with their cathedral. In the case of York, the ambition was to combine the existing Minster Library with a relocated Diocesan Registry and Record Office in Dean's Park. The proposal was financially supported, initially, by the Pilgrim Trust, and the Minster's architect, Sir Alfred Richardson, was charged with working it up into a costed plan. Only in 1948 was the question of funding for the reinstallation and restoration of the Minster's windows taken up in addition.[14]

Most unusually, Milner seems to have taken his "eye off the ball" in relation to the combined scheme with the diocese. Richardson developed an ambitious project including a two-storey building at a cost well beyond anything anticipated by the Pilgrim Trust, or possibly by Milner himself. When this became obvious, the Trust was very clear that it would only fund what had been already agreed, and that the scheme would have to be reduced considerably in scale and cost. This only became apparent at the point when Milner was also seeking Trust support for the reinstallation of the windows.[15]

It was a tricky period, both for the Minster and for the Trust, as it became more and more clear that the Trust could not, and would not, fund all the requests coming from parish churches and cathedrals. Faced with this situation, a radical rethink was required, prompting Milner's abrupt personal decision in early 1949, and without any consultation with the archbishop, the diocesan registrar, or his own chapter colleagues, to withdraw the Minster from the proposed partnership with the diocese. In an already febrile situation, it was a risky move. But in reporting the dean's actions to his trustees, Kilmaine suggested there was little that the

---

14   LMA/Pilgrim Trust Minutes/1948.

15   LMA/Pilgrim Trust Minutes/1948.

Trust could do but accept what was a fait accompli. Otherwise, it risked putting in jeopardy the Trust's priority to the Minster's glass.[16]

However blunt, Milner's arbitrary decision removed any ambiguity. It was recognized that the project would be a long one, not simply because of its scale, involving some 80 windows in total, but because it included some of the greatest examples of medieval glass in the Christian world. The Trust was confident that it had the funds; what was not clear was whether the very particular craft skills needed were sufficiently available, given that no new apprentices had been taken on since before 1939, and training for this kind of work was lengthy. This was also to assume that there was sufficient technical expertise, historical knowledge, and materials to support such an endeavour. For most of the period from 1945, the Minster could only call on two specialist and experienced Minster staff, the elderly Herbert Nolan and Oswald Lazenby, who were joined by a young apprentice, Peter Gibson, in 1948.

The contract of 1948 reflected these realities, combined as they were with continuing rationing of critical resources including petrol, materials, transport, and other goods and services. The agreement, which proved the prototype for periodic three-year reviews and renewals for the next 15 years, was that the Trust would pay the wages of the specialist artisanal staff, while materials and other costs would be raised elsewhere, including a public appeal. It was a very skilled and adroit arrangement, possibly unique at the time; whether it was formulated by Milner, Kilmaine or collaboratively is not known, but it served its purpose well.[17]

Once the Trust had agreed to support the reinstallation and restoration of the Minster's windows in phased stages in 1948, it was unswerving in its commitment, with Kilmaine regularly writing to Milner reassuring him that the Trust wished to see the project completed fully, and as speedily as possible, drawing down future anticipated financial support if required. In response, Milner was scrupulous in keeping Kilmaine fully apprised of progress, which could be passed on to trustees, and in a subtly different formulation to his annual reports to the Friends of York Minster.

---

[16]   LMA/Pilgrim Trust Minutes, especially 2/2/1949.
[17]   LMA/Pilgrim Trust Minutes/4450/A/01/012–016.

Kilmaine could be so confident not because he dominated his body of trustees, whose long-serving chairman was the kind of man who was quite prepared to give clear instructions to the secretary, if he thought it necessary. Much more significant was the great confidence Kilmaine had in Milner himself.[18]

Kilmaine well knew that the Trust had in Dean Milner-White a man who would be, in today's language, chairman, chief executive and project manager (or master glazier as he called himself) for the project, an authoritative expert in the field, at no additional cost to the Trust—a benign coincidence, not without its operational drawbacks. It was this unique set of circumstances that encouraged Kilmaine to try to speed up the completion of the programme, as Milner moved into his seventies, and was visibly weakening from 1960. If he died or was forced to retire, it would create many delays and dilemmas. Milner was also very aware of this and fully supported the plans to create a York Glaziers Trust to continue his work, although determinedly not letting go of the reins in his own lifetime. Once again supported by the Pilgrim Trust, the founding of the York Glaziers Trust proved to be a less controversial legacy. It was opened in 1967.[19]

To summarize a complex set of actions, it would not be true that much later criticism of Milner's achievement is simply anachronistic. Ever since William Morris's diatribe "Anti-Scrape" in 1877, discussion of the preservation and restoration of historic buildings has been in continuous dialogue about what should be the most important informing principles in what has become a global "heritage industry". There were choices 70 years ago. Milner made those choices unilaterally because, as Sarah Brown and others have put it, "he knew he was right". While at times

---

[18] For Kilmaine/Milner-White mutual confidence, see Kilmaine to Milner-White, 25 May 1960 and 8 November 1960. Milner, however, remained very clear that he was not going to give up the reins, and early in 1962 described himself as in the "Highest Spirits". Pilgrim Trust papers LMA/4450/A/01/012–016/Trust Minutes, LMA/4450/A/03/Secretary's Papers.

[19] York Glaziers Trust, "Our Story", <http://yorkglazierstrust.org/about-us/our-story/>, accessed 3 October 2024.

this can be explained operationally, as we have seen, it also reflected his temperament—he assumed command in the trenches, the Fellows of King's left the college chapel largely to him, his personal determination led him to select the sort of men he preferred, and he was prepared to use his own wealth to get his own way—all played their part. As we have seen, it had been his inflexibility as Superior of the Oratory of the Good Shepherd in the 1930s that made its evolution more painful than it might otherwise have been.

He could also be ungracious and self-regarding in the way he treated colleagues, while also securing considerable devotion from others, especially those younger men he had appointed. Not all his geese turned out to be swans. Others, while respectful, saw his faults, especially as he grew older. Even those who managed their relationship with him skilfully, like John West-Taylor, did not entirely trust him. He also became increasingly intransigent about contemporary scholarly research in the study of ecclesiastical glass, calling much of it "rubbish" in an address to the Council for the Care of Churches in 1956 on "God, Truth, and Beauty".[20]

Finally, he failed to give full credit where it was due. In his annual reports to the Friends of York Minster, it is noticeable that the Pilgrim Trust is lightly acknowledged for its generosity, whereas his letters to Kilmaine are expressed very differently. This side of his personality is particularly seen in his relationship with the Canon Precentor, Frederick Harrison (1884–1958), as gently expressed many years later by Peter Gibson, one-time boy apprentice, later wholly responsible for the Minster's glass. Harrison had been a residentiary canon since 1925 and was a learned man, particularly on the Minster and its glass, writing the definitive study of it in 1928. Gibson commented that Harrison deserved to have been consulted more on the restoration of the Minster's glass, but did not elaborate. This would seem to be a fair, if unspecific, comment, as Milner must have used Harrison's work extensively in terms of his own education on the glass on arrival. One wonders why Milner behaved in this way. From an obituary tribute to Harrison on his death

---

[20] Eric Milner-White, "How to Choose Stained Glass" (London: Church Information Office, 1959).

in 1958, they were clearly very contrasting clerics, with Harrison being a hearty, convivial, uxorious man, given to mimicry, very different from a mannered aesthete interested in "beautiful" things. The two men had known of each other for a very long time, as Harrison, from a provincial grammar school, had also gone up to King's to read history in October 1903. They were exact contemporaries, but there is no evidence that they moved in the same circles and Harrison was awarded a third rather than a double-first. Perhaps he knew more about the dean as a young man than Milner was comfortable with.[21]

From 1957, Milner was becoming increasingly frail. By about 1960, he had to use a wheelchair on occasion, a fact later reported by Kilmaine to his trustees, a development deeply worrying to the trustees as well as to the city and the Minster. If Milner had to retire or were to die, the Pilgrim Trust's continuous commitment to the Minster's medieval glass over the previous 12 years might be at risk.

He had a major operation in 1961, but recovered, recording himself as "fighting fit" in November 1961, but at some point, he was diagnosed with terminal cancer.[22] In civic terms, his attention focussed on providing the city and the Minster with a scholarly Glaziers Trust able to build on what had been achieved since 1941. The decision of the UGC in April 1960 to found one of the first "new" universities at York added unexpected possibilities, of enabling the city, Minster, and university to collaborate in the history, conservation and understanding of stained glass, locally, nationally, and potentially internationally—one element in Milner's ambitions for the city in the fields of the decorative arts.

While absolutely determined to keep personal control of the Minster's glass in his own lifetime, these succession plans, fully and creatively encouraged by Kilmaine and the Pilgrim Trust, were reasonably well advanced at his death. At the same time, he gifted much of his own collection of paintings, pots and books to the City Art Gallery, the Minster Library, and the future University Library. To paraphrase the

---

21   KCAC for Harrison's obituary, *King's College Annual Report*, November 1958. For Peter Gibson's later comment, Peter Gibson, "A Treasure House . . . ", in Holtby (ed.), *Milner-White: A Memorial*, pp. 59–91.

22   On Milner's declining health, see Wilkinson, *Milner-White*, pp. 42–3.

title of his lecture to the Friends of Gloucester Cathedral in 1952, that a cathedral should be a "home for all the arts", so he wished that his adopted city should be an inspirational home of learning, preservation, conservation, the applied arts, crafts, and beauty.

1 3

Milner, the diocese of York, and the wider Church, 1941–63

Milner did not play a leading part in diocesan affairs, partly by tact, partly by inclination, nor did he directly encourage the parochial clergy to see the Minster as part of the integrity of the diocese. He discontinued, for instance, inviting prominent parish priests to preach at the Minster. The one notable exception was the Diocesan Advisory Committee, the body responsible for granting "faculties" to individual churches to alter their buildings, fittings, and furnishings, as well as the external environment of churchyards and burial grounds.[1]

Among Milner's early colleagues was Canon England, who as well as being canon treasurer since 1933 was also chairman of the Diocesan Advisory Committee (DAC). Canon England died in late 1944. Rather unusually, Garbett, as archbishop, appointed Milner as his successor, a diocesan office he held until his death. Usually, the post was offered to one of the diocesan archdeacons. Milner accepted immediately and it was clearly a position he enjoyed, rarely missing its cycle of monthly meetings at the Deanery. The committee had an influential membership of diocesan representatives, including the diocesan registrar, suffragan bishops, and archdeacons, as well as experts, professional and scholarly. As well as sanctioning an application from a parish, it might well have to broker agreements between patrons, incumbents, parochial church councils and their church wardens, as well as local opinion. It involved regular parochial visits in the more significant or contentious cases.

---

[1] Borthwick Institute for Archives, Diocese of York Papers, YDA/3—Diocesan Advisory Committee Minutes, 1944–63.

The appointment of the dean of the local diocesan cathedral was not common, but comprehensible in the case of Milner, who had been a member of the diocese of Ely's DAC. Given his conviction that churches, large and small, should be places of spiritual "beauty" in terms of worship, liturgy, music, and as a potential home for "all the arts", his role within the widely scattered diocese of York could be significant. What would also have attracted Milner to the role was that it enabled him to build on his ambition for the city and diocese to become a centre for art, craft, and conservation with a potentially national and European reputation, as it had been in the late Middle Ages, in his opinion. As we have seen the length of his tenure also gave him the opportunity to promote the work of artists that particularly attracted him. Additionally, the range of the decisions his committee had to make casts a further light on Milner's principles on church restoration and enhancement. It was also indirectly a commentary upon the creative and imaginative approach adopted in the case of newly built or highly damaged churches like Coventry Cathedral or Eton College Chapel. By looking at these many local examples, we can see that Milner's priorities were liturgical, aesthetic and creatively traditional, as well as being more generally consistent with the historical documentary record.

Inevitably, much of the business was routine. Not surprisingly, immediate decisions had to be made about the war memorial boards and about adding electric lighting and heating. Typically, the DAC took these things seriously in respect of materials, positioning, and design. It was clear that the persons being commemorated should always have their first Christian name included, and that the phrase "To the Glory of God" was not appropriate. On lighting, concern about style and materials was important; plastic shades in Bakelite were not acceptable.

In addition, the faculty system had significant weaknesses. One was that there was no requirement to seek relevant and qualified architectural advice *before* the application was submitted, an inefficiency that clogged up the system. In general, it could not be guaranteed that the relevant archdeacon was necessarily adequately informed or skilled enough in advising individual parishes about how to present their best case. The church architect George Pace (1915–75), who had recently relocated with Milner's encouragement to York, had become a member of the York

Diocese Advisory Committee in about 1950, and thought that the system needed more architectural input. His recommendation was that there should be a five-yearly diocesan inspection of each church's condition, which was accepted and subsequently implemented across all dioceses in 1955.[2]

More significant schemes, including new churches, major modifications or new furnishings, windows, or chattels, involved complex negotiations between often strong-minded parties. Broadly speaking, Milner and his colleagues supported regional architectural practices, craftsmen, and glass painters with well-regarded reputations, although there were exceptions. The most notable was the agreement that Selby Abbey could accept the gift of a statue by Sir Jacob Epstein, *Ecce Homo*, even though to some it did not have an explicit Christian message. For other reasons, it was never installed.[3] In another case, at Boynton, just west of Bridlington, Milner and his colleagues robustly rejected the proposal of the local patron for new glass as totally inappropriate.[4]

---

[2]   George Pace (1915–75), Who was Who; Wikipedia; Peter G. Pace, *The Architecture of George Pace, 1915–1975* (London: Batsford, 1990).

[3]   Selby—the background to this is that Epstein's *Ecce Homo* was sculpted in 1934–5, but remained in Epstein's possession. In the mid-1950s, a local person in Selby wrote to Epstein to say it could be wonderfully placed in Selby Abbey, but there was no means of purchase. Epstein and his wife decided to come to Selby and view the abbey. As a result, they gifted the work to the abbey. This required the necessary faculties and so came to Milner and his committee, who approved the application. This is interesting as an example of Milner's discrimination in terms of modern ecclesiastical art. The engaged citizens of Selby were less happy, with some 400 objecting that the representation of Christ was grotesque or monstrous. The diocesan chancellor vetoed the plan owing to the local opposition. In 1969, the statue was given to Coventry Cathedral, where it remains.

[4]   Boynton—it is clear from Pevsner that the DAC's imperious rejection of the dominant patron's scheme meant that the church retains its special eighteenth-century integrity. Nikolaus Pevsner and David Neave, *The Buildings of England: Yorkshire: York and the East Riding* (London: Penguin Books, 1972), pp. 333–6.

As a result, it exercised a discreet patronage of favoured artists—Harry Stammers, George Pace, Francis Johnson of Bridlington, and Robert Thompson of Kilburn. Milner was able, through his personal enthusiasm for glass painter Harry Stammers, who he had encouraged to relocate his studio to York in 1947, to show his own priorities in the creation of newly commissioned church glass in worship, instruction and prayer, as well as his own scepticism about new fashions in the prestigious post-war commissions at Coventry and Eton College.[5]

In the case of new or war-damaged churches, the decisions also involved other bodies—the Archbishop of York, in the case of new churches, and the civic authorities in that of St Martin le Grand, Coney Street, York. Usually, if the proposed scheme was generally acceptable, the committee supported the suggestion of architectural practices such as those of George Pace, or those of Francis Johnson (in Bridlington). Pace largely fashioned the new church of the Holy Redeemer in Acomb, which combined some of the more ancient stonework taken from the ruined church of Bishophill Senior with the modern windows created by Harry Stammers, which later received the positive approval of Pevsner.[6]

In the case of workers in wood, the committee steered applicants or donors towards Robert "Mousey" Thompson (1876–1955) of Kilburn and were beginning to commend the young Dick Reid (1934–2021). Few differences of opinion are recorded in the minutes.

But the one area in which Milner clearly led the committee, unsurprisingly, was in relation to contemporary church glass, and his personal enthusiasm for the work of Harry Stammers, (1902–69), who he had directly encouraged to move to York in 1947, with the dean and chapter providing the premises at the Minster for his studio.

Milner disliked much of the now most famous stained glass of the period, such as that of John Piper in Coventry Cathedral or that of Evie Hone and John Piper in the new east window of Eton College Chapel,

5   Henry Hinchcliffe, *The Stained Glass of Harry Stammers* (Mindelph Press, 2016), pp. 8–11; 296–7.

6   Pevsner and Neave, *The Buildings of England: York and the East Riding*, p. 160. Entry on the Church of the Holy Redeemer, Boroughbridge Road, York.

which had been lost through war damage.[7] During Milner's tenure as chairman, Stammers was the glass painter chosen by the York DAC in over 30 cases, as well as those in which he collaborated explicitly with George Pace. Not widely recognized at the time, Stammers' reputation has been transformed by the excellent study of his work by Henry Hinchcliffe in 2016.

What was it in a Stammers window that so appealed to Milner and his colleagues? In very broad terms, they obviously told a Christian story, both scripturally and in relation to daily life, both contemporary and historical, often within an appropriate local context or referencing a specific trade. Milner specifically recommended as an example the Stammers window at St Wilfrid's, Ottringham, and that of St Mary's, Scarborough. At the same time, in answer to an apparently unsolicited enquiry from the Revd J. N. T. Boston in respect of his church of St Nicholas at East Dereham in Norfolk, Milner replied with great thought and sensitivity.[8] Inevitably in a large corpus of work, not all his work was equally regarded by the DAC, but only very occasionally did they ask Stammers to suggest amendments or modifications.[9]

But in Milner's own case, two personal elements came into play, each illustrated much earlier in his life. The first is Milner's admiration for the work of the hymnodist and liturgist, the Revd Percy Dearmer (1867–1936), the radical vicar of St Mary's, Primrose Hill, with his deep commitment to Christian Socialism.[10] Dearmer had composed a Litany to Labouring Men (date of composition not known) to be used on appropriate worshipping occasions. In his chapter on worship in *The Church in the Furnace* (1917), Milner recommends its use, although

---

[7]   John Egerton Christmas Piper (1903–92): *ODNB*, vol. 44, pp. 396–8; Eva Sydney Hone (1894–1955): *ODNB*, vol. 27, pp. 897–9. For Milner's opinion on the Eton Chapel, Pare and Harris, *Milner-White: A Memoir*, p. 32.

[8]   For the text of Milner's reply to the Revd Boston, see Hinchcliffe, *Harry Stammers*, p. 9. For the resulting window, see p. 140.

[9]   BIA, York Diocese, Diocesan Advisory Committee, Minutes 1944–63. For details of Stammers' commissions within the diocese of York, Hinchcliffe, *Harry Stammers*, pp. 311–13.

[10]   Percy Dearmer (1867–1936): *ODNB*, vol. 15, pp. 652–3.

there is little evidence of its being taken up. But in churches in which a Stammers window had been installed, there was hardly any need, as his figures, biblical and contemporary, visually demonstrate the nobility of male and female labour. For such churches, it was not necessary to intone a Litany of Labour as it was before all worshippers visually every Sunday.

The second example is not a Stammers window, but the window scheme introduced by Milner into the new modern church in Bitterne in the 1920s as a memorial to his father. What we see in the stained glass of the only parish church in which Milner had almost a free hand, and well before he became acquainted with the work of Stammers, are realistic scenes from the Scriptures along with episodes from the history of Southampton. In his much later handbook on choosing stained glass, written to support diocesan advisory committees around the country, Milner commends the Bitterne scheme, without mentioning his own personal connection with the church.[11]

In conclusion, Milner's nearly 20 years as chairman can be seen as a success from the committee's minutes. Milner had a deep knowledge of almost all things relating to churches, historic and contemporary, he chaired the group sympathetically, and his own views were very rarely at total variance with those of the other members. The committee made clear decisions, both positive and negative, and it encouraged artists, architects and craftsmen of quality and imagination in the diocese, and more broadly in Yorkshire. If Milner had an agenda both for the Minster and the diocese, it was that they should restore their late medieval reputation in these fields, an ambition linking all his involvements with Anglican churches whether parochial, diocesan, or national.

A poignant final personal example is to be found in his last attendance in 1961 at a full governing body meeting at King's College, which had been such a formative influence on him for 60 years. On that occasion

---

[11]   Eric Milner-White, "Churches, Artists and People", in the *13th Report of the Central Council for the Care of Churches* (London: Church Information Office, Church Army Press, 1959). Subsequently distributed by the Church Information Board later in 1959, under the title "How to Choose Stained Glass (Advice on Planning and Commissioning a Design) to assist Diocesan Advisory Committees".

he voted in favour of lowering the floor to accommodate the wonderful Rubens above the high altar, shocking scholarly purists in relation to the early sixteenth-century chapel. For Milner, beauty was superior to what he would have called antiquarianism.[12]

---

[12] Jean Michel Massing, "The Altarpieces in the Chapel of King's College, Cambridge", in Massing and Zeeman (eds), *King's College Chapel 1515–2015*, pp. 123–6.

Beyond the diocese, 1941–63

Among the many bodies of which Milner was a member, mention will be made of just a few in which he played some part. He was on the advisory board of the Victoria and Albert Museum from 1943, a member of the Alcuin Club, president of the Bradshaw Society (1943–58), a member of the literary subcommittee preparing the New English Bible and doubtless others.

Among this range of involvements, a number stand out.

The care of historic churches

During the immediate post-war years, new planning legislation was introduced in relation to historic buildings, of which the Town and Country Planning Act 1947 was the most important. While churches and their immediate grounds had some exemptions, it was widely accepted that churches and dioceses had to take equivalent actions. Archbishop Fisher, particularly, was very reluctant to take any corporate responsibility, hoping that the government would take the load (hardly realistic in 1948) or that some new body would be created specifically for this purpose, or that each diocese would have to muddle along as best they could. This procrastination irritated the Pilgrim Trust, which threatened to stop making parochial grants unless the Church itself had its own operational policies, and it was a possibly carefully inserted debate by the well-known activist on these matters, Ivor Bulmer-Thomas, at the meeting of the Church Congress in 1951, that led to the setting up of a working party. Bulmer-Thomas subsequently chaired the working party, of which both Milner and Seiriol Evans, now Dean of Gloucester, were members, writing its final report. This led to the modification of the Central Council for the Care of Churches. It is no surprise that Milner was appointed a trustee of this modified national body, with his earlier pupil and friend before 1914, Seiriol Evans, as the chairman.[1]

By 1950, Milner's experience in relation to churches, cathedrals and collegiate buildings was probably unique at the time. Not a person generally to put his head above the parapet, he certainly never committed to a full study of the Minster's glass or its post-war reinstallation and restoration. During his time, he would have had to rely on Canon Harrison's work in the 1920s, as presumably Pevsner also would have done in the first edition of his *Buildings of England* in 1972, devoted in part to the city of York. Even so, Milner did publish some individual papers for a defined readership, including a handbook on *How to Choose Stained Glass* (1959), a reprint of an earlier paper for more general use by diocesan advisory committees. From the tone and language of these writings and addresses, certain themes emerge which also help add to our understanding of Milner's personal approach to his "heroic" project at the Minster.

An early pair of these occasional papers date from 1950 and 1951. The first is Milner's account in the *Antiquaries Journal* on "The Restoration of the East Window of York Minster", which concludes with the following: "In a sentence, our motto has been, RECOVER DESIGN, PRESERVE TONE AND QUALITY" (Milner's capitalization).[2] The second is his address on "The Function of Colour and Design in Glass". In talking about ecclesiastical glass, he insisted that stained glass was "decoration" and that it should be seen as "architectural" NOT "pictorial", essentially glass "painted on light"—echoes here of the Fitzgerald memorial window in King's Chapel.[3]

---

[1] For the complex evolution of this body, see Lambeth Palace Library, List Archive Collections.

[2] Eric Milner-White, "The Restoration of the East Window of York Minster", *Antiquaries Journal* 30:3–4 (London: Society of the Antiquaries of London, 1950), pp. 180–4.

[3] Eric Milner-White, "The Function of Colour and Design in Glass", in *Report of the British Colour Council, 6th Designers Conference, York, 1951*

The second pair of addresses were delivered to the Central Council for the Care of Churches in 1956 and 1958. The first, entitled "Goodness, Truth and Beauty", had as its core that "God is Beauty", with one of its historic expressions being the creation of great churches. From Milner, this is not a surprising summation. The founding of the Friends of York Minster in 1928 identified its purpose as adding "beauty" to the Minster, and in his first address to the Full Chapter of the Minster in the spring of 1942, Milner had identified this as one of his own ambitions for York. The second of the pair was entitled "Churches, Artists and People", which had as its focus the question of what were the essentials in devising a scheme of enhancing a church with additional glass, an address subsequently published in 1959 as a guide for diocesan advisory committees. The first essential related to the function of a new window, in which for Milner "Art is always subservient to frame". The second was to understand the strengths and weaknesses of stained glass as both art and craft, which needed to acknowledge that stained glass was a "mosaic" art form, painting "on light itself". The third essential for sponsors was the choice of artist, on which, unsurprisingly, Milner recommended consultation with the local DAC. Finally, there was the question of the choice of subject for the window. On this Milner declared that no subject that "borders on the sentimental" is appropriate to the "powerful mosaic of stained glass".[4]

Post-Reformation saints

This apparently arcane issue, already mentioned, was expressed through his interest in whether the Anglican Communion should be able to create post-Reformation saints. This was a subject that had surfaced among the churches in East Africa in the late 1920s, and upon which Milner had written three feature articles in the *Church Times* in the following decade.

(Beaconsfield: Amberley Press, 1951).

[4]   Eric Milner-White, "Churches, Artists and People", subsequently distributed by the Church Information Board later in 1959, under the title "How to Choose Stained Glass (Advice on Planning and Commissioning a Design) to assist Diocesan Advisory Committees".

After 1945, the question returned with Archbishops Fisher and Garbett establishing a clerically composed commission to consider the issue thoroughly in 1948. Milner was asked to chair it, along with the young Eric Kemp, later long-serving Bishop of Chichester, as its secretary—both Anglo-Catholics with a strong historical knowledge of the western Church.

It proceeded in a considered and leisurely fashion, reporting in 1956, two years before the Lambeth Conference of 1958. Its unanimous report was short, lucid, and well written, including how the Anglican ecclesiology might be deployed in changing environments over time.[5]

It had most probably been the product of both men. It was anchored on the historically sound premise that the early Christian Church was highly local in its first centuries, with considerable elements of diocesan autonomy and diversity in the hands of its bishop. As far as the western Church was concerned, this was self-evident in the Celtic regions in the continuing dedications of its churches to local saints in Cornwall, Wales, and Ireland. The spiritual primacy of the church of Rome, and the unique position of the papacy, only slowly extended across western Europe following the Gregorian reforms of the early Middle Ages. Thinking about sanctity and the potential creation of saints also gradually evolved, culminating in the Council of Trent, by which time new forms of religious autonomy, spiritual and territorial, had evolved in western Europe during the Reformation. As for the English Church, both catholic and reformed, a distinctive ecclesiology had emerged, expressed politically through the separation from Rome by Henry VIII, the Elizabethan settlement, and the Restoration in 1660, and in the philosophical, scriptural, and spiritual writings of Richard Hooker, Lancelot Andrewes, and the Caroline Divines.

Within this overarching framework, a variety of ways of celebrating the Church's "heroes" had been sanctioned in the Kalendar of the BCP across the Christian Year (Red and Black Letter days). Because of the strength of religious feeling prompted by the Reformation, the issue of

---

[5]   The commemoration of saints and heroes of the Faith in the Anglican Communion: the Report of a Commission appointed by the Archbishop of Canterbury (London: SPCK, 1957).

creating post-Reformation saints in non-Roman Catholic environments was hardly contemplated before the 1920s. By that time, the nature of the global Christian Church had totally changed through the spread of temporal empires—British, French, Dutch, Spanish and Portuguese— altering structures of Christian churches, especially those maintaining a "catholic" ecclesiology. For the Roman Church, the Vatican Council of 1870-1 brought to a high point the spiritual authority of the pope and the curia with its now highly regulated and hierarchical pathway towards "sanctity".

The "Milner" Commission's report was judicially balanced. Respectful of earlier views on the past-history of this issue, it stated that whatever level of "heroic" esteem was being sought from the variety of situations within the Anglican Communion, locally generated enthusiasm was a necessary pre-condition. Within this inclusive framework, the locally appropriate bishop also had to endorse the degree of recognition for local "heroes".

This suggested approach was accepted within the Church of England, being later incorporated within the agreed resolutions of the Lambeth Conference of 1958 representing the Anglican Communion globally (Resolution 79).

In what may seem to the contemporary reader an academic discussion of the worst kind from a different age, featuring in no headlines at the time, it may nevertheless have provided a validated way of future thinking.

Originating in the late 1920s among the bishops in colonial Africa, at that time largely white, it enabled locally distinctive Anglican practices to evolve, whereby locally "heroic" Christian lives could be recognized and memorialized. Perhaps surprisingly, it also provided an uncontentious context for agreement in the Anglican Church in New Zealand in 1991 to form a union between the three Anglican traditions in that part of the Communion—English, Maori, and Polynesian.

The Liturgical Commission

The second contribution to the wider Church came from Milner's membership of the re-established Liturgical Commission initiated by the two archbishops in 1955 (Fisher and Ramsey). It was not a happy experience for Milner, leading to his resignation on the issue of the liturgy in relation to baptism in 1960. Under the chairmanship of the Dean of Lincoln, D. C. Dunlop (who had also been a member of the Milner Commission on post-Reformation saints), it had quite a turbulent history, being put into a state of animated suspension by both archbishops in 1960, only resuming its work in the following year under a new chairman, Donald Coggan, recently appointed Archbishop of York. Milner was probably uncomfortable with the proceedings from the beginning, but it was the discussions around the baptismal liturgy that agitated him particularly, bringing out some of his best qualities and his worst.

The Christian "sacrament" of baptism is one of the two most important, and has been a matter of theological, historical, and practical debate from the earliest years of the Christian era. For the western Church, the practice of infant baptism with witnessing godparents and later adult confirmation had become general practice by the early Middle Ages, only to become again the object of much debate at the time of the Reformation, with dissenting churches practising adult baptism with full immersion as scripturally authoritative. Cranmer's Book of Common Prayer broadly retained existing catholic church practice. Milner had long thought that reform of the baptism service could have been one of the positive achievements of Prayer Book reform. With the rejection of the legislation in 1927 and 1928, he had written his own version for voluntary use in the Northern Province, authorized in 1951, although its subsequent popularity is unclear. The reconstituted Liturgical Commission selected baptism as one of its first areas of consideration, thereby providing the opportunity to discuss Milner's liturgy, and potentially extend its authorized use. But its conclusions were not unanimous, with two members, including Milner, producing a dissenting minority report.

It had also produced tensions between the chairman and Milner, with the former suspecting that Archbishop Ramsey was working in collusion with Milner, possibly correctly. It was all very unfortunate and may have contributed to the decision to suspend operations for a period, and secure a new chairman in 1961, by which time Milner had resigned from the Commission. Putting aside the merits of Milner's own Northern Rite, and there were critics, his own disillusion with the proceedings stemmed from a belief that the Commission was taking a too scholastic approach, and was not sufficiently historically appreciative of the development of child baptism since the Apostolic age in the western Church. Unsurprisingly, he was also not keen on what was seen as the kind of contemporary language to be inserted into the Book of Common Prayer. The issue fizzled out and, by the time the Liturgical Commission submitted its own final report in 1966, Milner had died.[6]

The Church and Anglican education

Milner's last campaign in the wider church was in connection with Woodard Schools, of which he had been provost of its northern chapter since 1945. At present, the author has not been able to track down any material relating to the northern chapter, although there is doubtless some at the individual schools. Milner's own papers have very little, other than very late in his life in relation to the establishment of two new Woodard schools near Southport (Brantwood School for girls) and at Tynemouth (King's School for boys). This chance opportunity seems to have energized the already sick dean, especially that of the King's School, Tynemouth. Both were existing proprietary schools whose owners wished to retire, which Milner saw as an opportunity to extend Woodard provision in the north. The story of King's School is best told by its first headmaster, almost certainly appointed by Milner, the Revd Malcolm Nicholson (King's and Cuddesdon), in his insightful and sympathetic tribute following Milner's death. The foundation by the Revd Nathaniel Woodard of a structure of middle-class Church of England schools,

---

6   Eric Milner-White, "Two Proposed Orders for the Baptism of Infants: A reply to Professor Ratcliff", *Theology*, November 1960, YML SC Pamphlet Box 158/15.

inspired by Anglo-Catholic principles from the 1850s, of which Lancing College is the leading example, was clearly Milner's ideal.[7]

The introduction of school education as one of the final strands in this study may mystify the reader, but it has a purpose of opening another of the more contradictory elements of Milner's character; that of national education. No Anglican priest, after the 1840s, could deny that Christian instruction and education were central to the mission of the "national church", especially for a man closely connected with schools and colleges—King's College, Cambridge and its undergraduates, working-class schooling in Southwark, teaching young choristers at King's, and as chairman of the governors of St Peter's School in York, as well as taking a prominent part in promoting the civic case for York having a university from 1942 until 1960.

But alongside this, a less sympathetic profile can also be put. In south London, despite his close friendship with Arthur Wayment, his neighbour in Woolwich and head of a new London County Council elementary school, he seems to have had no opinions on how the English state should try to reconcile the need for a national system of education with existing denominational provision at all levels. For a church historian, this was remarkable.

Some of these contradictions are the more surprising after he came to York. By chance, through his invited membership of the Civic Committee, he would have received many of the various proposals about post-war education in York, elementary/primary, secondary and tertiary, once the school leaving age had been raised. In this context, the future of Archbishop Holgate's Grammar School, founded in 1546 as a civic grammar school seems to have engaged him less than the pattern of cooling towers on the aesthetic of the city a few years earlier.

Following the passing of the 1944 [Butler] Education Act and its implementation, Milner's influence could have been significant, but he chose not to use it, possibly prudently if unadventurously, as Chairman of St Peter's School. He did not support the changes in status of Archbishop Holgate's Grammar School in 1945 and would have preferred the school

---

7   For Woodard Schools, see Wikipedia entry and <https://woodardschools. co.uk/about-woodard/>, accessed 4 October 2024.

to become wholly independent, believing that it would offer a better education than the compromise sanctioned by the local authority. As far as is known, he took little interest either in the restructuring of elementary/primary education in the city, despite its being a critical issue in national education since before 1870.[8]

He was, unsurprisingly, a supportive chairman of the independent St Peter's School on Bootham. Even in actively supporting the idea of a university at York, his approach was curiously idealized. He knew almost nothing about any university, outside King's and Cambridge, in that order. In addressing the York Rotary Club on education in 1942, his talk had little that indicated any knowledge of contemporary thinking about national education. Furthermore, there are brief passages in Milner's only and co-authored novel, *The Story of Hugh and Nancy*, which are patronizing and condescending about local Board schools.

It is striking that one of the residuary beneficiaries of his will was the northern province of the Woodard Foundation.[9]

---

[8]   Ernest Norman Jewels, *A history of Archbishop Holgate's Grammar School, York, 1546–1946* (York: Archbishop Holgate Society, 1963).

[9]   For details of Milner's will, see *Church Times*, 28 February 1964, p. 15.

Milner-White: Private passions, aesthete, churchman, and lover of "All the Arts"

As this study comes to its conclusion, it is important to add what we can about Milner the private person, despite his vigorous efforts to cover his tracks by destroying the overwhelming bulk of his private correspondence. Nevertheless, he left traces, which can make up a tentative assessment.

In his personal decision to become a priest, following his visionary experience in the autumn of 1905, there was a partly formed commitment to celibacy. There was no deviation from that throughout a long life. This can be seen in the inner debates he had both from 1912 and again in 1918 on whether he should join the Community of the Resurrection at Mirfield in West Yorkshire, as well as the critical pledge to celibacy in the principles of the Oratory of the Good Shepherd. Like many men of his class who were unmarried, his company was largely made up of men, outside his immediate family, in both work and leisure.

He was shy in female company, but not hostile to it, and could be charming in their presence, as was shown in greeting his godson, then an undergraduate at New College, Oxford and later prominent in government during Mrs Thatcher's premiership, and his future wife for an overnight stay at the Deanery in 1962 during their vacation hitch-hiking tour.[1]

Similarly, he was clearly fond of Erica Pare, a family friend who became his housekeeper, assistant, and executor in York. Late in life, Milner became interested in the garden of the Deanery, focussing on

---

[1] Private information.

roses and heathers—Erica being the Latin name for heathers. Similarly, that ability to charm can be seen in the numerous women of a certain class agreeing to donate their pre-war ballgowns and fabrics, vestments, and *objets d'art* to "beautify" the Minster. On the relatively few occasions when girls were present at the choir camps at Batcombe, there were affectionate later accounts.[2] Finally, Lydia Lopokova, the wife of John Maynard Keynes, was an important influence in converting Milner to the ballet after 1930.

Among young men at King's, he could be painfully shy—a puzzling trait after four years in the trenches—well known for chronic silences with undergraduates outside the chapel circle. In that context, his persona changed markedly, as evidenced in the large number of undergraduates who became ordinands at Cuddesdon under his influence. As with many Anglo-Catholic celibate priests, fellow priests predominated in his daily life, as his visitors' book of his time in York testifies. But he did not develop close male friendships with men of his own generation. This was partly accident. His closest friend as an undergraduate, Philip Loyd (1884–1952), fellow Trappist, also later a priest, with whom he took European holidays up to 1914, eventually went to India and became later the first Bishop of Nasik before returning as Bishop of St Albans in 1944. Milner wrote a warm tribute about him for Loyd's biographer.[3] He later acquired and installed in the Minster a fine seventeenth-century Dutch window taken earlier from a church in Rickmansworth in his memory. Among other early friends, Gerald Fitzgerald, an exact contemporary at Harrow and King's, also reading history, had been killed in 1915, and Arthur Edghill had died in an accident at a Boy Scout camp in August 1912.

Among priestly friends, Milner preferred to work with younger men, his "Benjamins", as one of them described himself as the headmaster priest of King's School, Tynemouth. As we have seen, this was to be his last "crusade", and he devoted his fast-dwindling energies and personal

---

[2] Mary Holtby, "Childhood Memories . . . ", in Holtby (ed.), *Milner-White: A Memorial*, pp. 43–5.

[3] R. P. Stacy Waddy, *Philip Loyd: Missionary and Bishop* (London: Mowbray's, 1954), pp. 19–22.

wealth to the project. Milner, as was noted above, was notorious in appointing King's or at least Cambridge men to posts that he could influence. Outside the Minster community, Seiriol Evans (1894–1984) was probably his closest clerical colleague. A former undergraduate at King's before 1914, while Milner was chaplain, it was Evans who provided the earlier vignette of the overnight boat trip to Ely and climbing into the close at daybreak. By the early 1950s, Evans was Dean of Gloucester, inviting Milner to address the cathedral's Friends, which he did as we have seen under the title of "A Cathedral—Home of All the Arts". Both men were trustees of the Central Council for the Care of Churches, of which Evans was chairman (1954–72).[4]

But it was among children that Milner seemed often to be the most at ease, shades of his vision in 1904. His annual Choir School camps at Batcombe in Somerset between the wars were clearly one of the high points of his year. But he was also very talented as a classroom teacher at King's College School in his divinity lessons and in preparing boys for confirmation, among whom the most revealing is the young Michael Ramsey, who comments in his own epilogue to the Pare and Harris memoir in 1965, and included as an appendix to this study. They remained in contact throughout his life, with many of Ramsey's major published works in Milner's own collection including warm dedications, to which Milner replied movingly.

Turning to Milner's own enthusiasms. As a schoolboy and undergraduate, he was a keen sportsman, especially in cricket, which remained a life-long passion. He played for the adult male choir in Woolwich, and at King's would don his old blazer to play in the annual match against the choristers. He was a member of the MCC, usually attending the Lord's Test, and it was a matter of pride that late in life Colin Cowdrey's name appears in his Deanery visitors' book.[5] From his first year at King's, his interests turned in a more artistic direction and he started going to the opera at Covent Garden, often alone. He heard many of the great pre-war singers perform. Visits with Philip Loyd around the

---

[4]   Seiriol John Arthur Evans (1894–1984): Who was Who.

[5]   Milner's Deanery Visitors' Book, YML, Milner-White Papers, 6/1 (2 April 1960).

cathedral cities of Europe often included the local opera house. They were in Oberammergau for the 1910 performance, Milner retaining his programme. There is less evidence of this after 1918 until the late 1920s, when he substituted the ballet, also in London, which became a passion, attending nearly 900 performances over the next 30 years, again preserving all his programmes. These he had bound in annual volumes held in the Deanery and deposited in the special collections of the Brotherton Library of the University of Leeds on his death. It is surprising that he came to the ballet so late in life and he owed a great deal for that to Lydia Lopokova, Keynes's wife. She was a dancer with the Ballets Russes, and is said to have later commented that English ballet did not need a "choreographer" as they already had, in Milner, someone with a way of orchestrating Special Services that had all the holistic elements of movement, space, light and music of any professional choreographer.[6] For Milner, ballet became his passionate dramatic art, combining as it did music, movement, drama and the human form.

The other main artistic passion of his middle and later life was collecting modern twentieth-century Japanese "studio pottery", of which he had the largest collection outside Japan at his death. These included artists such as William Staite Murray, Bernard Leach, Reginald Wells and Shoji Hamada, then not well acknowledged as outstanding in their sphere. It is a puzzling choice for a man seemingly conventional, even cautious, in his artistic tastes. Nevertheless, in writing about his collection in the 1950s, it is very clear that he saw ceramics as the most superior decorative art form, in terms of "beauty", that essential quality of the aesthetic sensibility. Milner, by his own later account, was introduced to twentieth-century studio pottery in 1925, describing his "conversion" experience as follows:

---

[6]   Wilkinson, *Milner-White*, p. 15; YML, Service Orders, 6–2–2–20—Epiphany Processions with Carols (1947). This was the first use of Milner's Special Service for Epiphany with its Service Order, explaining its liturgical structure and scriptural narrative of the Three Kings, as well as the choreography of the choir's (*corps de ballet*) movement around the Minster's space, for which it had been specifically designed.

> It was by pure chance c.1925. I walked into a Bond St. Gallery
> (the Fine Art Society) and saw a show of stoneware pots by Reg
> Wells. Transfixed. Sat for two hours—forgot lunch!

He bought his first pot. Thereafter it became the single most important aspect of his personal collecting. A wealthy man since 1922, he assembled a trail-blazing collection, which became the largest in private hands in Britain, including significant works by the artists mentioned above. Murray and others later commented on how important Milner had been for them through his patronage.[7]

As with so many aspects of his artistic taste and patronage, Milner did not write very much about his pots, but he did write the introduction to an exhibition of his collection in the York City Art Gallery in 1952, which gives some clue. In this brief piece, Milner identifies the four aesthetic elements in judging the quality of a pot as FORM, GLAZE, DECORATION and SURFACE, which created for him the criteria of the pre-eminent of the decorative arts, a synthesis of painting and sculpture.[8]

Milner had added to his wealth by the death of his mother in 1951 and for the remainder of his life was a very active purchaser of paintings and pots.

Initially, he seems to have intended the bulk of his ceramic collection to be gifted to the Fitzwilliam Museum in Cambridge. But the relationship did not develop in ways that Milner endorsed and, with his increasing enthusiasm for his adopted city, the York City Art Gallery, as well as the Southampton City Art Gallery, were to be the home of his pots following his death.[9]

---

[7]   Sarah Riddick, *Pioneer of Studio Pottery: The Milner-White Collection*, introduction and catalogue (York City Council, 1990), p. 9. Sarah Riddick's catalogue is the definitive study of the collection, which the author has been privileged to have drawn upon with gratitude.

[8]   Riddick, *Pioneer of Studio Pottery*, p. 130.

[9]   Helen Walsh, "On What to Look for in a Pot", presentation at the Milner-White seminar, 2016.

Milner began modestly buying pictures from 1918 onwards, largely for his own pleasure. His choices were eclectic, largely the painters of his youth, Sickert, Whistler, Tonks, and Wilson Steer.[10] Unlike his enthusiasm for contemporary Japanese stoneware, his taste in pictures was more conventional, never abstract or avant-garde, but could be modern as in the case of Stanley Spencer and Eric Gill. After 1950, his picture collecting took on a different profile as their numbers increased, aspects of which, in Richard Green's view, are a little difficult to untangle in any individual case.[11] There were purchases which he thought would give him continuing personal pleasure, there were those that he would enjoy for a time and then donate, and finally there were those purchased specifically to enhance a public collection well known to him. Undoubtedly, his move to York encouraged this development. He was quickly asked to join the city council's committee on the City Art Gallery in 1942 and became enthused particularly following the appointment of a new director, Hans Hess, who, as we saw earlier, brought a new dynamism to the institution from 1948, something capitalized on during the Festival of Britain in 1951. The gallery was to be a major beneficiary of Milner's generosity.

In addition to pots and pictures, Milner was an avid bibliophile and collector, with interests in all aspects of their production—paper quality, print, binding, and book plates all featured, echoes possibly of the salon world of Charles Sayle in Cambridge between 1903 and 1907. It is significant that he insisted that the Minster's own Special Service sheets should be of high quality in terms of weight of paper and distinctive typeface, and of aesthetically pleasing design.[12] He may well have passed on this concern to John West-Taylor, founding registrar of the university,

---

[10] Sarah Riddick, "The Dean as Collector", in Holtby (ed.), *Milner-White: A Memorial*, p. 46, fn3.

[11] Richard Green at the Milner-White seminar 2016 at the University of York.

[12] An examination of the early service order sheets from 1942 to 1947 shows that Milner kept his own copy, having each of them finely bound (by York printers H. Morley), usually individually, with leather spines and highly decorated boards in an "Arts and Crafts" style, very similar to the approach adopted in the *Letters of Hugh Stanley Wilson*, edited by Geoffrey Keynes and Cosmo Gordon (anonymously), and published privately in 1920.

who was adamant that all university-headed notepaper, notices and the boards to which they were pinned should have a common design and style in terms of typeface, with blue borders and blue-covered drawing pins.[13] It may not be a coincidence that both men in different generations had been friends of Henry Morris. All three men contributed in different ways to the overall aesthetic of the university in its original development plan, and the choice of Matthew/Johnson Marshall as the university's architects.[14]

Milner's own library, many of whose volumes contained his own bookplate in the style of Eric Gill, was professionally wide-ranging, but also contained much contemporary English literature, including Masefield, Drinkwater, Auden, Fry and Eliot. It is interesting that Milner seems never to have connected with Eliot, even though the poet's adoption of Anglo-Catholicism, as well as his later plays and essays on culture, share some of Milner's own assumptions. The much earlier *Four Quartets*, of course, had contained the poem entitled "Little Gidding", mirroring Milner's own fascination with Nicholas Farrer and his community in the same place. Milner's library came to York Minster Library and the University of York library on his death and deserves more scholarly study. It contains over 2,000 books, including many by the Catholic modernists of the early twentieth century, especially Father Tyrell, the Caroline Divines, and on the decorative arts. Intriguingly, there are almost no books on ballet.

The last of Milner's "private passions" was the detective novel of the interwar ("Golden Age") period, of which he had a large collection of first editions, numbering hundreds, kept in a separate room in the Deanery, and not for loan.

If one volume only were presented as bringing together his bibliographical and aesthetic interests in books, it might be the limited

---

13   Personal knowledge.
14   Robert Matthew Johnson-Marshall, see Colin Marrs, "RMJM'S York University buildings listed", *The Architects' Journal*, 24 August 2018. This was the first of the four campuses designed by RMJM, inexplicably not mentioned in the Wikipedia entry.

edition of the Gospels, scripted and illustrated by Eric Gill, purchased in the early 1930s and now in the Minster Library.[15]

Nor does this exhaust his artistic and aesthetic interests. Milner joined the Advisory Committee of the Victoria and Albert Museum in 1944, he chaired the Henry Bradshaw Society from 1943 with its interest in and publication of historic Christian liturgies, and was a member of the Alcuin Club with its focus on contemporary liturgy. He had considerable knowledge of ecclesiastical metalwork and wrote a pamphlet on work done in the Minster under two former deans, Foxley Norris and Ford.[16] His taste for enhancing the Minster's furniture tended to be conservatively contemporary, with works by Richardson, Tapper and Peers.[17] In relation to his own purchases for the Minster or gifts accepted, not all won approval; their volume, like his prayers, inevitably, were varied in quality and beauty. As earlier, if one had to identify a single example of Milner's mixture of talents and approaches, it might be the set of very fine Jacobean silver altar candlesticks bought independently by the elderly Earl of Halifax, for the high altar to complete his earlier memorial to his father, the 2nd Viscount, carried out in the late 1930s. It was noted earlier that the 2nd Viscount had been the leading Anglo-Catholic layman in the Church of England within the English Church Union from the 1880s until his death in 1934. The gift put Milner in a dilemma, which he disguised in the carefully expressed replies to the earl's munificent gift, of which in terms of quality and beauty there could be little doubt. But as Milner explained, the numbers of candles on a high altar, especially one so magnificent and important as at York, could be misinterpreted by low churchmen and evangelicals for whom two candles only were seen as obligatory. The compromise agreed was very typical of the dean: the candles would be in place at services attended by representatives of

---

15   *The Four Gospels of the Lord Jesus Christ, according to the Authorized Version of King James I*, with decoration by Eric Gill (Waltham St Lawrence: Golden Cockerel Press, 1931).

16   Eric Milner-White, *The wrought-iron work of the Minster* (York: The Friends of York Minster, c.1950).

17   Irvine Watson, "Some major furnishings introduced under Dean Milner-White", in Holtby (ed.), *Milner-White: A Memorial*, pp. 39–42.

other Christian churches, but for the daily office, the regular two would be used. This would not only be suitable for such special services, but would reflect the 2nd Viscount's lifetime commitment to the catholicity of the whole Church.[18] On the earl's death in 1957, Milner orchestrated the requiem mass in the Minster, which was the model for his own in 1963, on his instruction.[19]

---

[18]   The Halifax Candles, YML, Milner-White Papers 2/8, especially Milner-White to Halifax, 4 July 1957. Both Halifax and his father, the 2nd Viscount, had known Milner well, initially as lay supporters of St Anselm's and the Oratory of the Good Shepherd in 1919 and 1920.

[19]   Memorial Service, Wilkinson, *Milner-White*, pp. 42–3.

16: New church at Bitterne (above); Bitterne, Window in the new church (below)

17: Rouen Window, sixteenth century, acquired by St Mary's Church,
Rickmansworth from St Jean, Rouen; later removed and in store in 1952.
Purchased by Milner-White and installed in York Minster [window s6]
as a memorial to his friend Philip Loyd and his brother, Lewis

18: Harry Stammers in his workshop

19: Window in St Nicholas, Withernsea, East Yorkshire (1947);
Stammers comments, "The feelings in play here; Jesus' compassion,
the woman's contrition ... are almost palpable."

20: *Window in St Nicholas, Hollym, East Yorkshire (1948); an unusual example of Stammers making full use of clear glass, allowing the visual context of the church to be internally and externally illuminated*

21: *St Andrew, Bishopthorpe, York (1950); "The Church as provider of education throughout the ages" (Harry Stammers)*

22: *St Matthias Church, Stocksbridge, South Yorkshire (1950); "My brothers the birds, much ought ye to praise your Creator" (Francis of Assisi)*

23: St Martin's Church, Firbeck, Nottinghamshire (1953); Six parables in glass

24: St Helen's Church, Welton, East Yorkshire (1954); "A celebration of Church music" (Harry Stammers)

26: St Michael's College, Llandaff (1959); a unique example of Stammers'
work in a new church and in collaboration with George Pace

25: Christ Church, Wadsley Bridge, Sheffield (1957); "A Litany of
Labour in glass", the panel directly reflecting agriculture and industry
in contemporary dress, rather than the complete window (opposite)

27: *York College for Girls, York, North Yorkshire (1960); "The third shepherd, with the red cloak, is a portrait of Eric Milner-White, Dean of York. This window is now in the Merchant Adventurers' Hall, York." (Harry Stammers)*

28: *North Riding Mental Hospital, York (1949); a moving institutional tableau in glass, now poorly re-instated in the Chapel of York District Hospital*

1 6

Last years and valedictory address
to the Church Union, 1962

Milner was 77 in 1961 at the time of the Kents' royal wedding and already
a sick man, with Kilmaine reporting to the Pilgrim Trust in 1960 that
he was much reduced, but in no mood to hand over his control of the
Minster's glass. He continued actively as dean until a few months before
his death in June 1963, planning an opening service in the Minster for
the "new" University of York scheduled for the following October, and
composing what was his final prayer for the fish-porters of Billingsgate:

> O Lord Jesus Christ, who after Thy glorious resurrection didst
> prepare by the waterside a breakfast of fish for disciples that had
> toiled the whole night long: come amongst thy servants who toil
> beside our river day by day to provide food for their fellow men,
> and bring Thy blessing both on their work and on their lives, O
> Lord our Saviour and help for evermore.[1]

Milner died on 15 June 1963, just two weeks after the death of Pope John
XXIII. Their lives had coincided in time very closely and were devoted
to their individual versions of Christian Catholicism.

During this final year of his life, Milner chose to give a valedictory
address at the annual meeting of the Church Union. A 40-minute address
on how the Church of England had changed in form and practice over
the period of his life, it is the only recorded version of any of his addresses

---

[1] Pare and Harris, *Milner-White: A Memoir*, p. 44.

that is known to have survived.[2] His analysis was surprisingly upbeat, in which the catholic elements within the Church seemed to Milner to be converging, following the pope's announcement of his summoning of a Second Vatican Council in 1959, almost immediately after his election.

Milner reviewed the progress of the Anglican catholic tradition within his lifetime from the early 1880s. Before 1914, he characterized parish worship as overly Sunday-focussed, with its high point as Matins with sermon. The Eucharist was in the margins, said usually at an early hour, except for the major festivals in the Kalender. By 1960, he saw Anglican practice as in rapid evolution in a more sacramental direction, with a Christian life being spread more across the week in parishes, cathedral worship and colleges, along with more frequent celebrations of the Eucharist at accessible times as well as a greater use of the reserved sacrament. This had been accompanied by additional music, both choral and instrumental, along with movement and the singing of hymns, all of which had featured in his chapter on worship in *The Church in the Furnace*. Worship in parishes would reflect local custom and the constraints of the building, but he noted the increasing impact of the Parish Communion movement and the popularity of harvest festivals and Mothering Sunday since 1900. In large parish churches, cathedrals, and other venues, he had seen a growth in Special Services often of a national and civic character, or where a Christian-inspired body might celebrate its achievements, formally rededicating themselves in terms of their own ideals. He had shown both at King's in the Festival of Nine Lessons and Carols and in the National Days of Prayer, as well as in York Minster, his own talent in constructing services of this type.

At the same time, he had appreciated the impact that broadcasting and film could have on moulding "national character" in human history, which he had affirmed in 1904 as an undergraduate historian. His was not a global perspective in relation to other faiths or Christian denominations, or towards a more socially and politically engaged Anglican Church, as was Archbishop William Temple's. Nor was it inclined towards negotiated convergence between Christian churches, whether Roman Catholic or

---

[2]   BL Sound and Moving Image Collection, C1305/28/2—Address to the Church Union 1962.

Reformed. His vision in these areas was more anchored in an ideal of the common catholic unity of the Christian faith, sacramental, universal, and mystical. His overall optimism lay in the potential released by a renewed Vatican tolerance of what he would have called "Modernism" in 1914 in the writings of Teilhard de Chardin and Hans Küng. Both his life and that of John XXIII had stretched between Vatican Councils and it is historically ironic that they died within weeks of each other in the early summer of 1963.

Concluding personal summation

Researching and writing about the character, life, and career of Eric Milner-White, a notoriously secretive, private, and shy man in adult life, has had elements of the detective novels he so avidly read. His destruction of all his family and personal papers in the years before his death in 1963 has compounded the challenge, as has the range of his interests and activities. As outlined in the introduction, this created a problem for the Sheldon Memorial Trust initially in finding a person to give a public lecture in York and then to write a publication. When, in the tradition of revivalist meetings, no one came to the front, the chairman of the subcommittee had to step up to the mark. This is the result.

In this final concluding chapter, I want to achieve four things. Firstly, to fill out our knowledge of that life, as there were only memorial tributes in the public domain. Secondly, to consider his achievements and failures during his own lifetime. Thirdly, to assess Milner's personality and the balance of his qualities, given that he divided opinions during his own lifetime. Finally, 60 years later, does his life have any significance in the vastly changed landscape of the Church of England today?

Filling in a concealed life

1884–1907

As with most biographical studies, the early years of a subject's life are contextual, on occasion qualifying that context, as in this case.

Milner was born into a recently successful business family from the Isle of Wight. By good fortune, Henry White, Milner's father, had been privately tutored by the headmaster of the local school in Cowes, which enabled him to go to Cambridge and read law. In addition, Henry's sister had married into the leading private retailing company in Southampton, Edwin Jones, who had no sons. Lacking an obvious solution, Edwin Jones invited Henry to join the family business, of which he became managing director and chairman after Edwin Jones' death. It had been a rapid rise by Henry into the provincial haute bourgeoisie, unusually a high church Anglican in Christian practice and joining a Southampton family that already had a leading profile commercially and civically. Conscious of their rapid rise socially, both Henry and later Milner were also very aware of social difference.

With that background, it was predictable that Milner should gain entry to Harrow School, whose pupils were a mixture of new wealth and sons of aristocratic families.

Unlike his later situations, Milner was positive but not lyrical about his time at the school. An able boy and a successful cricketer, only his history tutor seems to have had a significant impact, encouraging Milner's talent with words and the study of the past. Probably expecting to follow his father and uncle to Pembroke College, Cambridge, he won a scholarship to King's College to read history, a relatively new single-subject Tripos at the university.

This proved to be one of two pivotal moments in his life, with his going up in October 1903 to King's, one of the leading colleges, recently separated from its fellow royal foundation, Eton College. It had an informal atmosphere in its relations between dons and undergraduates, of which Milner took full advantage in his first two years with apparent changes in his character noted by fellow undergraduates who had known him at Harrow.

His tutor, Oscar Browning, was one of the most powerful influences. Browning was a leading and controversial personality in Cambridge at the time, with his distinctive mode of teaching through the Political Society, which he had founded in 1880. Milner and Browning got on well from the start, with Milner becoming secretary of the society in his third year. Through its minutes, we gain some idea of Milner's youthful opinions on the political and historical questions of the day. In addition, Browning's informal "salon" held in his spacious rooms enabled selected undergraduates to mix with his exotic and wide-ranging contacts outside

Cambridge. The impact of this environment was to encourage Milner's artistic and aesthetic enthusiasms, often with its homoerotic ambience, in which the similar "salon" of the scholarly bibliophile librarian Charles Sayle and his Baskerville Club probably also played a part. A natural potential member of the secret society the Apostles, Milner was not invited to join as he remained a devout high churchman, becoming a member of another secret but religious college society, the Trappists, whose members watched his transformation with insight and discrimination.

If these elements were not enough, Milner secured a double-first in the history Tripos, as well as continuing to play more than simply cricket. He over-stretched himself, having a "frightening" religio-psychological episode in the autumn of 1905, including a "vision" of Christ walking among London street-boys, which led directly to his decision to become a celibate priest.

It has been important to provide this context and personal background to Milner's early life as it was largely ignored by his earlier memorialists because of his close friendship with his tutor, Oscar Browning, up to 1914. But he had made his mark among his contemporaries and among the dons through winning the Lightfoot University Prize in Ecclesiastical History, which may also explain how he was invited to return to King's as chaplain in 1912 after four years in Southwark.

Not all warmed to him or his "style" at that time, and the ambiguity was well expressed by Merlin, head Trappist, who made the comment in 1903 or 1904 that Milner "wishes to aspire and does not mind the consequential fall. As a brother he has a very good opinion of himself." It was an insight that could apply to the whole of Milner's later life.

But there is another element to this individual story in that it extends our understanding of what was of some significance in the history of the university before 1914. In addition to the pervading agnosticism or atheism of the Apostles, with the young G. E. Moore of Trinity at its core, there was in the same decade a religious energy among college chaplains and undergraduates, which was to contribute to the distinctive Anglican tone of the university, both before and after the First World War, later identified by Archbishop Michael Ramsey in 1965.

Nevertheless, the principal aim in this account of Milner's early life is to fill in some of the gaps, resulting from sensitivities felt by memorialists soon after his death, and from Milner's own decision to destroy all his personal archive in his lifetime.

1907–18

On leaving Cambridge to train at Cuddesdon in 1907, there was little significantly out of the ordinary in his early clerical career in Southwark in two well-known Anglo-Catholic parishes, predominantly in Woolwich, with a single personal exception. This was in the figure of Arthur Edghill, an older contemporary of Milner at King's, where he had been a scholarly phenomenon, and a possible Trappist before being ordained. However well they had known each other at that time, they reconnected simultaneously in 1908 when both arrived in Southwark, with Edghill becoming sub-warden of St Saviour's College, the settlement attached to St Saviour's church, the designated cathedral in the new diocese. Edghill was an important influence on Milner, not only because of his frenetic energy, but because of his intellectual power as a theologian and historian of the early Church, and his passionate commitment to the work with boys. This was particularly expressed in his enthusiasm for the recently founded Boy Scouts, with their outdoor emphasis, their undogmatic Christian ethos, and Edghill's and others' almost mystical belief that God was working through the new movement. It echoed Milner's earlier frightening vision of the autumn of 1905. He felt acutely Edghill's accidental death at a Boy Scout camp in August 1912, something later expressed in a letter to the retired Browning as chaplain at King's. In surveying the evidence of Milner's period in south London, it is confirmatory of the later revisionist writing on the impact of the settlement movement in S. C. Williams' important study of religious practice in Southwark in this period.

On his return to Cambridge in 1912, Milner was still uncertain of the direction of his priestly life as between education or the monastic. What was clear was that it was unlikely to be in the parochial ministry.

In the four years outside Cambridge, much had changed in the theological atmosphere within the colleges and among their chaplains following Pius X's blunt attack on Catholic Modernism in 1908. As the new chaplain of King's, and inspired by John How and others, Milner threw himself energetically into a collective attempt to modify existing college worship away from a routine pattern of Sunday observance, trying also to deepen the Anglican life of the university through the establishment of a university-wide Anglican centre devoted to the catholic English tradition, initially called St Anselm's. Stalled by war from 1914, Milner became critical in what became the Oratory of the Good Shepherd in 1919 and 1920 and its prior, following the unexpected death of J. N. Figgis. It became the first example of the way Milner worked for the rest of his priestly life. As John How commented at that time, it was not so much that he supplied a detailed scheme, more that Milner brought an enthusiastic energy and a "vision" for realizing an aspiration in a form greater than that originally hoped for. Sometimes, as in the case of the Oratory, that "vision" became impossible by the early 1930s as the context had changed, with much personal agonizing. As Sarah Brown has commented, one of the more challenging aspects of his personality, as well as the positive, was that "he knew he was right".[1]

As earlier in Woolwich, there was nothing out of the ordinary in Milner's response to the outbreak of war, volunteering as a temporary chaplain and serving continuously until late 1917 on the Western Front, later destroying all personal records of that period particularly. He was a brave man, winning the DSO in 1917. From other evidence, we have some private letters describing the agonies of battle and a brief extract from his account of life behind the frontline, which is beautifully written. More significant in the longer term was his individual chapter on "Worship and Services" in the edited volume *The Church in the Furnace*, published in 1917. Written in exceptional circumstances, it turned out to be the foundation statement of what unifies essential parts of his later ministry. Reduced to its bare bones, it was that the 1662 Book of Common Prayer in all its aspects needed reform to make it "more homely" for the bulk of the population on a regular basis, without diluting its authority or the grace of much of its language. Secondly, that large churches, cathedrals, and chapels needed carefully to reflect on their role in the nation's public religious life as the established Church, after the war, which should also

---

[1]   Sarah Brown at the Milner-White seminar in 2016 at the University of York.

include Special Services. This phrase was ambitiously interpreted by Milner at King's on Christmas Eve 1918 following the Armistice, in the later National Days of Prayer, especially in 1940 and 1944, and in York Minster from 1941.

1918–41

Elected Dean of King's in the early summer of 1918, Milner remained a college character for 23 years. Distinctive in dress, manner, and mode of speaking, he could be easily parodied, caricatured, and imitated, all of which may have been a carefully constructed persona hiding a basic shyness, outside the chapel community—all of which was recorded in the tributes following his death. But how did his life match with the outline of his earlier life, both within King's and Cambridge?

Almost immediately, his first Special Service on Christmas Eve 1918 was for the town of Cambridge as well as the college, it being outside the university term. As was to become a habit, an earlier idea was transformed by Milner in substance, and by his own bidding prayer, into something much more subtle than its Truro version in 1880. Circumstances, and the development of broadcasting, allowed it to become a national and global "beginning" of Christmas around the English-speaking world, an immediate outcome of the content of his essay in *The Church in the Furnace*. It was not easy to replicate within a collegiate and termly institution, but it could be stored for his new life in a leading cathedral setting after 1941.

Within Cambridge, his focus was largely collegiate, both in extending patterns of worship in a more sacramental direction, and through the writing of prayers and liturgical forms, although not hymns, over the next decade, in addition to taking charge of the Oratory of the Good Shepherd.

In the national Church, in which he had no official authority outside Cambridge, he was a prominent presence within the Anglo-Catholic renaissance of the decade, speaking at its congresses and writing articles on the nature of a historical universal catholicism of the Christian Church from the Apostolic age. These were particularly critical of Vatican and papal developments since 1870, which he saw as increasingly destructive of a more abstract and idealized, almost mystical, historical unity of the catholic Church. Reading this material for the first time, I was surprised that such opinions were so strongly expressed from within the Anglo-Catholic movement at the time. Not unexpectedly, he took no part in the Malines conversations or in the parliamentary politics in connection with the proposed revision of the Prayer Book. Rather, he jointly wrote, with Father Wilfred Knox, a polemical response to Father Vernon Johnson's account of his own conversion from his visit to Lisieux in 1925.

Milner similarly took little interest throughout the interwar period in the priorities of the Church of England as a whole, dominated as they were by archbishops Davidson, Lang and especially William Temple, with their concerns about politics, social conditions, the Anglican Communion, and international relations after 1933. From many points of view, including possibly that of Milner himself, he was sand-banked in Cambridge, moving gradually towards a comfortable retirement as an already rich man, following the death of his father in 1922.

As earlier, it was chance that changed that life story in 1939, as of course it did also that of fellow Harrovian Winston Churchill. Along with his winning a scholarship to King's in 1903, it was the other pivotal point, completely revitalizing him following his rather surprising appointment to the Deanery of York in 1941.

1941–63—the "civic dean"

For Milner personally, and for all those directly involved, it was a risky appointment, especially in an increasingly global war. Aged 57, he had almost no prior parish, diocesan, or cathedral experience, but it proved a creative move with Milner managing the Minster in his own very personal style, which today would be totally unacceptable. This included the extremely challenging restoration of the Minster's unique medieval glass in a post-war climate of severe continuing public austerity without seeking public funding. This he achieved over a 15-year period of skilful negotiation with the Pilgrim Trust. His first ambition in 1942 was to "beautify" the Minster itself, which he achieved largely through his sensitive handling of the Friends of York Minster, already firmly established. As at King's, he negotiated the Minster's music well with the two cathedral organists and masters of the choristers—Sir Edward Bairstow and Francis Jackson—promoting particularly the music of

Herbert Howells, which he greatly admired.[2] He was not always so careful, especially in his relations with his canon chancellor, Frederick Harrison, who certainly knew more about the Minster's glass in 1941 than Milner did. His treatment of Harrison was imperious and personal, especially as they had known each other as fellow history undergraduates at King's since 1903.

Milner's appointment as dean of the senior cathedral in the Northern Province gave him the scope to realize his vision for such great buildings in terms of Special Services as originally expressed in *The Church in the Furnace* nearly 40 years earlier, thereby enhancing the civic and religious life of the nation and its unique history—examples of which I have described. Once again, he opportunistically took advantage of the Festival of Britain in 1951 and the first royal wedding in the Minster since the fourteenth century to put both the city of York and its Minster, as well as Yorkshire itself, on the map of public consciousness in post-war Britain, from which much could flow.

Milner would not have known the city of York well before his arrival in late 1941. He had not travelled widely since 1918, rarely preaching outside Cambridge and London, nor taking many holidays around the UK or abroad. Moving to York was therefore a surprise, with him immediately and unexpectedly adopting the city as his new home, engaging with the life of the city, and presenting himself very much as a new citizen rather than the new dean. In so far as he had a model to follow, it seems to have been that of his father in Southampton as a leading citizen and churchman. Milner, as dean, was formally the permanent second citizen of the city to the annually elected Lord Mayor as first citizen. The dean, therefore, had a status in the city beyond the Minster, which he could develop. He did this with surprising skill and political sensitivity in relation to the other elected senior citizens, above all Councillor J. B. Morrell. It was a very productive partnership as Morrell similarly realized that Milner could be a great ally in his civic aspirations in creating the post-war "City of our Dreams", using his considerable authority in the city to involve the dean in building the York version of the "New Jerusalem" after 1945. This was to be pre-eminently through

---

[2]   Paul Spicer, *Herbert Howells* (Bridgend: Seren, *c.*1998), pp. 130–1.

the creation of the York Civic Trust with his ally Oliver Sheldon in 1946. In the post-war development of local urban amenity groups, preservation societies and conservation bodies, civic trusts were in many cases the most ambitious. In the case of York, it was one of the earliest and most successful. Within its voluntary, independent, and charitable structures, it allowed individuals, often influential, powerful, and knowledgeably interested citizens, to make their own civic contribution, without either becoming directly elected councillors or public campaigners. York was obviously a place that could support a civic trust, and it proved an ideal base from which a historically informed dean, with wide aesthetic and artistic interests, could play a significant non-political role, something of which both J. B. Morrell and Milner were aware. At times, it would not have been clear in which capacity Milner was working, whether as second citizen and dean or as secretary to the Civic Trust, an ambiguity within which he could enjoyably operate. The best examples of this were seen in the Civic Trust's work to support the development of the City Art Gallery, especially in his own role with the Friends of the Gallery, his support of the new curator, Hans Hess, and not least his increased personal generosity in the last decade of his life and in his will. The second Civic Trust project in which Milner played a major part was the campaign to secure a university for the city, an ambition first floated by Milner a few months after arriving at York in a talk at the local Rotary Club in 1942.

Curiously, it was the sphere of education for York's children that was a blind spot for Milner throughout his priestly life, in that he showed almost no interest in state education. This was despite the local authority's increasingly critical role after the Forster Act of 1870, as well as its being a vital part of Christian mission.

Milner was only really interested in independent schools such as St Peter's School on Bootham, with its historic connection with the Minster through which the dean customarily became the chairman of its governors, a responsibility assiduously discharged. Milner's real passion was for the schools of the "high church" Woodard Foundation, predominantly boarding schools, with Lancing College in Sussex as its flagship.[3] By 1945, the foundation had schools for boys and girls in the Northern Province, of which Milner had been the provost since 1945. The possibility of extending the provision of such schools in the North-East and in north Lancashire energized the now sick dean, confined to a wheelchair, as eloquently described by the Revd Malcolm Nicholson (King's Cambridge and Cuddesdon), first headmaster of King's School in Tynemouth, following Milner's death.

Despite this blind spot, it is fair to say that Milner fashioned a model of "a civic dean", that certainly worked for York and could do so more widely.

1941–63—the dean in the diocese

At first glance, Milner did not play a very public role in the York diocese, but appearances can deceive, as they did in 1944 when he was invited by Archbishop Garbett to chair the Diocesan Advisory Committee, which he did until his death. He clearly enjoyed it, and over that 19-year period he played an important part in the life of any parish that wished to improve or repair their church or grounds, which could only be achieved through a diocesan faculty issued by Milner's committee. Deans usually did not play this diocesan role, but it was an inspired choice by Archbishop Garbett, as in Milner he had a colleague uniquely informed on all aspects of church buildings, and with an aesthetic temperament that wanted to increase the "beauty" of every church, because, as he put it, "beauty" was of God.

His long tenure enabled him to make a lasting contribution to the spiritual fabric of the diocese throughout the North and East Ridings of Yorkshire following the advice given to an individual parish aspiring to enhance its place of Christian worship. He did this through the committee's patronage of artists and craftsmen, especially the glass painter Harry Stammers, Milner's most favoured artist. Long overshadowed by more abstract artists like John Piper, Stammers' sensitive realism told both a Christian story as well as a human story highlighting daily life touched by the church's location, building, history, and labour across the centuries, including the present. Whereas abstract painters could adopt a wholly secular beauty, Stammers' windows were beautiful, vivid, and taught a

---

[3] For Woodard Foundation, see Wikipedia.

Christian human story that could illuminate, inform, and console. His windows were placed in more than twenty York diocesan parish churches in what Jane Grenville, author of the modern "Pevsner" for the North Riding, calls a "golden age" of modern glass painting in the county.[4] In a few cases, these windows were combined with architectural work by George Pace who, like Stammers, had been encouraged by Milner to move his studio to York. The factor that united Milner's ambitions for the Minster and its diocese was that both should become internationally recognized in terms of church crafts and arts, as he believed the region to have been in the later Middle Ages.

Outside the city and the diocese, Milner took on many representative functions in Church and State. As well as being on the literary committee producing the New English Bible, he chaired the Commission on post-Reformation Anglican Saints, a work of assistance in the global Anglican Communion, and, less happily, the revived Church of England Liturgical Commission.

This book's filling out of the narrative of Milner's priestly life has hopefully given a more comprehensive account of his achievements, failures, and omissions, as well as thickening our own understanding of his life and time.

It only remains to try to describe a man whose personality and achievements continue to divide opinion more than 60 years after his death. It also enables us to ask the question does anything in what can seem a remote age still have a relevance today for the Church of England, its role in the United Kingdom, and the Anglican Communion as a whole?

Milner the man

In the introduction to this study, I commented that Milner divided opinion in his own lifetime, as illustrated by the opinions of two Archbishops of York, Michael Ramsey and John Habgood. I hope that what has followed that opening remark has been confirmed to the reader.

---

4   Jane Grenville and Nikolaus Pevsner, *The Buildings of England: Yorkshire, The North Riding* (Harmondsworth: Penguin, 1966), p. 89.

Can, in the light of my researches, any resolution be achieved? Reviewing his life, we can obviously see a complex man with many clerical aspects and a great range of enthusiasms, as well as a secretive nature. Does this suggest a hidden life, as we have seen in many other prominent men and women? From what I have been able to access (and nothing has been withheld), I have seen no hint of this. For whatever reason, it is plausible that at the dramatic moment in 1905 when he determined to become a priest, he also decided to be a celibate priest, something that much later was a key feature of the Oratory of the Good Shepherd, and still is. By the 1920s, he is seen as chronically shy, except among regular chapel attenders. This shyness disappeared in the company of children, including godchildren or among those attending Scout-like choir camps at Batcombe throughout the interwar years. He was not wholly at ease in female company, but not hostile to it as his relationships with Lydia Lopokova and Erica Pare show. If his life was dominated by male clerical colleagues, he preferred to have younger men working for him and with him, ideally from King's College or Cambridge more broadly. Many of these "Benjamins" later recorded great respect and affection for him, while not being unaware of his secretive manner of getting his own way.

His non-clerical enthusiasms as a rich man were by any definition eclectic, most obviously twentieth-century Japanese pots, classical ballet, contemporary detective stories, fine books, paintings, garden heathers and cricket. Other than those which expressed a whimsical or an eccentric side, most reflected his aesthetic character in adult life. "Beauty" was a word he deployed in many environments and could be seen in his changing manner and dress from his undergraduate years, which did not affect either a personal bravery on the Western Front or the respect of the troops for whom he was the "padre".

It was in his mode of his routine dealings with others that differences of opinion emerge. From an early age, Milner presented himself as a person quite pleased with himself, self-confident, possibly arrogant, which his academic success would have confirmed. In adult life that self-assurance could be positive, as evidenced in his bravery at the request of his platoon, recognized by his DSO, or in his energizing "vision" in fashioning the idea of an inter-collegiate Anglican institution in Cambridge into the Oratory of the Good Shepherd. But that same quality had its drawbacks in Milner's case. Having self-confidence is one thing, "knowing that you are right" is another. Combined as it was with a certain deviousness did not always build trust. In the case of the Oratory, it was combined with a stubborn "perfectionism" that did not help in the changed world of the 1930s.

At York, the challenges were very different, which overall Milner handled well, as we have seen, assisted as he was by a locally canny Alderman Morrell. Given his untypical induction into civic life in wartime, Milner was in a good position to work civically in ways that coincided with his own personality after 1945. This he did well through the Civic Trust, largely founded by Oliver Sheldon, playing an important part in giving Morrell's vision for York a reality, which included an important Minster dimension. He did much the same with his deep involvement with the art gallery, as well as in the long campaign for a university in the city.

As a pervasive presence in the city from at least 1951, he obviously attracted varying opinions, well-informed or anecdotal. Others may wish to follow up their own presumptions, but they can be crudely expressed by two persons of the period, one given to me personally:
Milner-White
"My ideal as a Dean".
The other,
Milner-White
"Dean of King's, and Queen of Deans".

What does the author think?

Each reader will make their own assessment.

Putting the negative first, I would not have liked his preciousness or the self-assurance that he was right, not just on matters of stained glass. I would not have warmed to his snobbism or his nepotism in appointing staff. Nor would I have endorsed his limited compass in relation to the wider Christian churches, particularly in the reformed tradition, or his condescending comments on other faiths. His apparent refusal to offer any opinion on contemporary affairs domestically, or internationally, is to say the least perplexing. In York, his lack of interest in the education of local children and young people was one of his severe limitations.

On the other hand, his destruction of all that he saw as personal to his life makes any character assessment very difficult. Unlike later critics, those who had worked with him closely or were inspired by him as undergraduates, ordinands or priests wrote with great affection, most notably Michael Ramsey. In trying to achieve a fair and balanced assessment, it is worth quoting three individual examples, each not well known.

The first is his very positive support and patronage of Harry Stammers. The second is his endorsement of Herbert Howells, whose religious music he admired. The third, similarly revealing, is his reply to a gift for the leading chorister from G. P. Brown, a branch librarian in Cheshire, who had written a spiritually reflective letter enclosing the prize. Each was expressed in a personal letter.

First is his advice, following a letter from the Revd J. N. T. Boston, vicar of St Helen's church, East Dereham, in Norfolk, on who to approach as an artist for a proposed window for his church. In recommending Stammers, Milner continued:

> He (Stammers) has a medieval mind, which rejoices in fantastic renaissance surroundings, which are alone enough to give distinction. A similar unusual imagination works on his subjects, which unites tradition, modernity, and grace . . .

Second is Milner's letter to Howells, after he had moved to York:

> By these last two services . . . I personally feel that you have opened a wholly new chapter in Service, perhaps in Church, music. Of *spiritual* moment rather than liturgical. It is so much more than music-making; it is experiencing deep things in the only medium that can do it.[5]

Third is his reply to G. P. Brown:

---

[5]   Spicer, *Herbert Howells*, p. 131.

As for your deeper question, the greatest gift of God to us in this life is the power, and the duty, and the reality, and the joy of living in the ETERNAL. Beauty in all its forms speaks an eternal voice, not only flowers, music, and the song of birds, but the lovely thought, and the thought and act of love. All these have an eternal value. They are part of our inheritance now, not a heritage that will come to us in the future. Much is to come to us in the future, but we have so much more now than most mortals allow their eyes to see and their hearts to understand.[6]

Milner-White today

Milner died over 60 years ago in what must seem to most readers a totally different age, simply of historic interest, given what has happened since. Does this study of his life offer any commentary on the dilemmas of the Anglican Church today and does Milner's Anglo-Catholic view and achievements provide anything of contemporary value?

Despite his many weaknesses and foibles, Eric Milner-White's career and achievements remain significant and relevant today, in my opinion. I would like to outline them in the following ways.

What was his definition of Anglo-Catholic, and does the designation Prayer Book Catholic still have significance today?

While never writing fully on his ecclesiology, Milner's definition of English catholicism (Anglo-Catholicism) is often not fully understood, even though it represented many of the views of the founders of the Oxford Movement. Today in popular usage, it is often seen directly as a product of that movement, especially as its impact spread to the parishes. As I have described, it has a much longer ecclesiological pedigree with a greater focus on the history of the early Church, the writings of the Fathers, and the religious writers of the sixteenth and seventeenth centuries.

---

6   Milner-White to G. P. Brown, 20 November 1954, YML, Milner-White 2/8.

Christianity is a historic faith and current debates need to reflect those 2,000 years, both events, traditions, and fashions, positive and negative.

Does Milner's interpretation of a "sacramental" universal catholic faith still have value in terms of potential Christian unity in a world more material and more aware of the contribution of all faiths?
In his valedictory address to the Church Union in 1962, Milner outlined the increasingly "sacramental" nature of Anglican worship during his lifetime, in both cathedrals and parishes. This has continued since his death at the same time as both the growth of a more secular world and a reinvigorated evangelicalism within reformed and independent churches in association with their own traditions.

In his more speculative writing in the 1920s, Milner expressed an almost mystical and universal "unity" within the catholic Christian faith, which he saw the Church of Rome as working positively against. His essentially late-Victorian philosophical idealism, in addition to Pius X's onslaught on Modernism, helps to explain his caste of mind, markedly different from many of his peers, particularly William Temple, with their concerns for domestic society and the international order. Milner's response to that was modest but significant, something recognized by Michael Ramsey—that all change had to be founded in prayer, especially within the Church. In addition, positive steps towards Christian unity could be more successful and visible through local practice, such as in the early Church service of agape, rather than ecclesiastical high-level diplomacy, more suited to the world of secular politics.

Are Milner's recognized talents in Anglican liturgy and the writing of prayers of continuing significance in worship within the Anglican Communion, along with the Book of Common Prayer?
As Milner himself recorded, he was trained at Harrow to write well, and he did so throughout his life. He also wrote many prayers to supplement the BCP and to construct new liturgies. He is often regarded today as antiquated or arch in style, but he wrote less preciously in letters or accounts where his purpose was different. For Milner, the BCP was a fundamental text for the Church of England and the interwar years were dominated by the 1928 Prayer Book, its parliamentary rejection, and

the fallout from it, with Milner contributing to its endorsed prayers, new or adapted. From 1939 onwards, he wrote for much wider local, national, international, and personal use. In these spheres, *Beyond the Third Collect* and *My God, My Glory* were the climax of this aspect of his life. For Milner, prayer was absolutely at the centre of his faith, and he recognized the challenge it posed the individual, as recorded in *The Church in the Furnace* in 1917, focussing on his phrase "the Loneliness of Prayer". Where skill in writing prayers is often in short supply today, he made a significant contribution.

Has the importance he attached to special services in the Anglican tradition in public worship any continuing civic value?

Milner never had any doubt that great cathedrals were part of divine creation, fashioned by mankind. For him, they were places for prayer and worship of universal significance. He was also aware of his unique good fortune to preside over two of the most beautiful in western Europe. With all his personal strengths and weaknesses, he grasped that responsibility with both hands, showing one of his enduring qualities, first identified by John How in 1912 on Milner's return to Cambridge as that of bringing "vision" to a partially formed idea.

One critical element in this brought together the religious and civic side of his character through Special Services, first identified in his chapter in *The Church in the Furnace*. Initially, I seriously underestimated the importance of 'Special Services' for Milner's definition of Anglo-Catholic worship. Milner was very impressed by Percy Dearmer's phrase that Anglican worship should be "Catholic, but English", combining as it did the narrative of the catholic faith with a historical account of England's story. It is ironic that, as he lay dying, he was planning the Special Service in the Minster for the opening of the new and secular University of York, but he died before he had completed the work. It was also an irony appreciated by both the incoming chancellor (Lord Harewood) and vice-chancellor (Lord James), who both commented on the oddness of the situation, as they were both no more than "agnostics" on matters of faith and religion.

Did Milner's increasing aesthetic persona have an importance still relevant for contemporary Anglicanism?

Throughout this study, I have emphasized Milner's artistic and aesthetic interests, especially in the decorative arts within a religious context. In talking to those who had known him later in life, I asked the question did they see him as an aesthete, which immediately prompted the answer, "Oh yes". This side to his character became evident as an undergraduate and was commented on by those who had been at Harrow with him, which to a degree prompted his crisis of 1905. Throughout his life the concept of "beauty" and "the beautiful" was frequently deployed. Not that there was anything unusual in this at the time in educated and artistic circles, including the Apostles.

Aestheticism was not for Milner a branch of philosophy; it was more a caste of mind with the idea of "beauty" as its informing principle. This was expressed in the liturgy of Christian worship, church decoration and conservation, and in his vision that cathedrals should be a centre for all the arts. We can see this as one of the connecting strands in the great variety of his interests and activities. He did not share the growing scholarly concern for historical integrity in the field of church glass restoration. More important for him was the beauty of the result, leading him late in life to support the lowering of the floor in King's College Chapel to accommodate Rubens' *Adoration*, much to some purist displeasure. For Milner, respectful and very well informed in almost all matters relating to churches and liturgies, "beauty" would win out against the "antiquarian".

In this context, it must have caused the undergraduates at King's some surprise to hear the dean extol in one of his last college sermons in 1941 not how they should develop their "character" as students (itself a cliché), but more that they should aspire to showing a "beautiful" character in adult life.[7]

Doubtless many of the dramatic changes in faiths across the world and in Christianity would not have been welcomed by the dean, but we should remember his valedictory address to the Church Union in 1962, which had an upbeat tone.

---

7   See above, p 53.

He would applaud the success of the English cathedral tradition, which sees much more engagement, and not just by tourists (who themselves should not be treated simply as providing much needed income), but also the popularity of regular choral evensong, special services, both Christian and civic, and national, along with the sense (not that he would have expressed it in this way) that civic life can be seen as moving through the cathedral.

He would also welcome the increase in the sacramentalism of regular worship and the critical role of prayer within the life of the individual and the Church.

He would commend the role of all the arts in parish churches as well as cathedrals and the ability of the Church to support talented artists. He would see the diocesan faculty system in combination with civic, conservation, and preservation societies as maintaining quality, beauty, and craft across the whole country.

For York and Yorkshire, he showed what it was possible to achieve as the dean of the cathedral, within the city and the wider region.

But perhaps we should leave the last word with Milner:

> Lord, let my reputation lie before Thine Altar
> and never lift itself up nor depart from thence;
> Lord let my life live in Thy sanctuary
> and move and have its being only there and thence.[8]

---

8   Pare and Harris, *Milner-White: A Memoir*, p. 92.

Seminar on Eric Milner-White, University of York, 2016

List of speakers and topics

- Peter Howson—retired army chaplain, Methodist minister, historian.
- The late Geoffrey Rowell—formerly the Bishop of Gibraltar in Europe, church historian and academic.
- Philip Williamson—retired Professor of Modern History, Durham University.
- Sarah Brown—Professor of the History of Art, University of York, and Director of the York Glaziers Trust.
- Richard Green—retired Curator of the York City Art Gallery.
- Helen Walsh—Curator of Decorative Arts, York Museums Trust.
- Katherine Webb—retired Archivist, Borthwick Institute for Archives, University of York.
- Peter Young—Archivist, York Minster Archives and Library.
- Christopher Collingwood—retired Canon of York Minster.

Epilogue by Michael Ramsey, Archbishop of York (1952–6) and of Canterbury (1961–74)

First published in Philip Pare and Donald Harris (eds), Eric Milner-White, 1884–1963: A Memoir *(London: SPCK, 1965).*

My memories of Eric Milner-White run through half a century from the day when I first attended his Divinity lessons as a small boy at the King's School till the day when I visited him at the Deanery in York shortly before his death. I knew him not as one of his most intimate circle but as one who was *very* conscious of his influence. He had a significant part in the life of the Church of England in this century, and it is about this significance that I write.

In the second decade of this century there came into being a Cambridge type (the word "school" would I think be too precise) of Catholic Anglican Churchmanship. It was an outlook deeply sacramental and devotional but intellectually more liberal than was common amongst the successors of the Tractarians. In the four or five years before the 1914–18 war there was a group of young high-church dons and graduates who were concerned to witness to Christianity in the University and to face the intellectual problems of belief in ways more modern than those of Bishop Gore and the writers of *Lux Mundi*, and were conscious of debt to the modernists in the Roman Church such as George Tyrrell. So began the Liberal Catholicism of which Sir Will Spens' book *Belief and Practice* (1915) was perhaps the most thorough-going expression. It was a Catholicism which put the weight of authority less upon the ancient Church and more upon the testimony of Christian experience through the centuries. Continuing in the years between the wars this Liberal Catholicism was best known from the volume *Essays Catholic and Critical* (1926), a product of scholars of several universities in which, however, the Cambridge outlook was very prominent.

The 1914–18 war, while it interrupted the Cambridge Liberal Catholicism as an academic, scholarly movement, gave immense impetus to it as a pastoral and evangelistic force. In 1913 John How, Eric Milner-White, and Edward Wynn had together founded the Oratory of the Good Shepherd as a brotherhood of celibate priests engaged in university work. Behind the Oratory lay the inspiration of the Little Gidding of Nicholas Ferrar and the Oratory of Cardinal de Berulle. But when the brotherhood settled down to its life and expanded its membership after the war there was no mistaking the influence of the war-time experience especially in the mind of Milner-White on his return from France. It is worth-while to quote from *O.G.S., A History of the Oratory of the Good Shepherd* words which Milner-White wrote in 1918 as an exposition of its ideals.

> The Oratory has been cradled in an historical epoch, which must largely determine its mission and labours. There are new needs to be met by the Church; and old needs, as yet unsatisfied by her, have been made visible to all eyes. Thus the sphere in which our little brotherhood is to work is marked by these outstanding characteristics:
>
> 1. It is a world tuned to high spiritual self-sacrifice for causes and claims, however sacred, less sacred than those of Christ.
>
> 2. A world in part ignorant of the Faith, in part with eyes directed on the verifiable facts of human truths; as a whole, blind to the Presence, even the use of Jesus Christ, and of any obligation to membership in His Church.
>
> 3. A world, therefore, eager to find occasion against those who openly profess Christianity: and finding it (a) in the scandal of Christian disunion and (b) in impatience of old definitions and ecclesiastical watchwords etc. which only irritate.
>
> 4. A world that, nevertheless, has seen and learned deep things, made new resolves, longs for brotherhood and for healing.

The Oratory, we hope, is to devote its life and energy in this new world, to the service of Christ in his Catholic Church. It is, in ideal, a close and loyal brotherhood of priest and laymen in the Church of England, which shall hold and live by the Catholic Faith in boldness and enthusiasm. But it is, at the same time, deeply conscious of a stewardship in a new and widened world: and so will make it a special study and fearless duty to welcome truth in all branches of thought, to meet modern thought and categories with sympathy in all its presentation of Christian teaching, and to refrain entirely from outworn labels and ecclesiastical catchwords which by offending the modern man or savouring of past controversies, are fit to die.

The Oratory must seek to fulfil a high ideal of self-sacrifice, and rival by a life of poverty and self-sacrifice, the death of that great company who sacrificed life for country in the Great War. It shall definitely tread in a way of the Cross. The outward sign of this shall be the common purse, strictly interpreted. More important shall be the corresponding spiritual effect of loving unselfishness.

Within the brotherhood, the Oratory shall present an example of a perfect family of Christian love. The spirit of love is to permeate every rule and every labour. Deliberate effort shall be made to heighten loyalty and love not only by rule, but by upholding the loftiest standard of fellowship and mutual self-surrender as a mark of the Community.

In the world outside, the brethren shall not only count every opportunity of unselfish action for the sake of others as a first duty, but also seek daily to make such opportunities. They shall be absolutely forbidden to speak scorn or ill of other types or bodies of Christians. So that in all things the practice of Christ-like love shall be the motive and method of oratory shepherdry.

To these ends the rule shall be made so severe as to necessitate every day a real effort of love on the part of each brother; and so light as will not enchain his charitable energy in the course of his daily round.

I have quoted this document fully because it reveals much of the mood and outlook of Milner-White in those early days. There was the enthusiastic and indeed romantic sense of opportunity which the war had left behind it. There was the call to sacrifice, and no less plainly the call to intellectual freedom and open-mindedness. Hence to many who were freshmen at Cambridge in the nineteen-twenties there was an awareness of a catholic movement of which the Oratory, with its mother house in Lady Margaret Road and its diffused work in a number of colleges, was the symbol. Here was a presentation of the Christian Faith emphatically Church of England in character but belonging to a wider Catholic Church, offering to our allegiance a disciplined and sacramental life, a call to sacrifice and service, and a conviction that the things of the mind are God-given and to be reverenced. Milner-White, shy and withdrawn from public activity as he was, seemed to be a power in the background, a symbol of a spiritual movement.

Milner-White shared no doubt in the enthusiasms of what was a school and a party, but with his great historical sense and his essential Englishness in character he could regale the trends of the time to historic Anglican tradition. That was his strength. His catholicism drew upon the sanctity seen in other Churches including the Roman, but it was nourished primarily from the Scriptures and the Anglican divines: the piety of Andrewes and Ken, the saintliness of Keble and King, the massive appeal to history of Dean Church and Bishop Lightfoot. His writings—apart from those on liturgy and prayer, of which I shall speak later—were not numerous and were chiefly "occasional", but they deserve to be recalled. There was his chapter in the war-time volume *The Church in the Furnace* (1917), his address on "Christian Unity: the Church of Rome" in *The First Anglo-Catholic Congress* (1920), his tract on *Ministerial Priesthood* (1923), his pamphlet on *The Value of the English Tradition* (1924), his essay on "The Spirit and the Church in History" in *Essays Catholic and Critical* (1926), and his joint work with Wilfred Knox *One God and Father of All*, a reply to Father Vernon (1929). These writings did not embody Milner-White's influence, which was always that of a counsellor and preacher rather than an author; but they illustrate it vividly, and their phrases recall the man and his impression.

Nowhere did Milner-White write more forcefully than in the address on "The Church of Rome" at the 1920 Congress. He saw already existing a true unity between Rome and Canterbury. There is the unity of many centuries of older history which they share; the dogmatic unity of the Creeds; the unity of sacramental life; the unity of saintly lives "in the priesthood, in the cloister and in ordinary walks of life"; and a unity of atmosphere which he calls "mystical" unity. Theologically this basic unity which persists despite divisions of polity, of doctrine, and of many quarrels is to be understood in scriptural terms as the unity of spiritual race, of the people of God.

> Remember Poland. Five years ago the Poles belonged to three great empires. Who will maintain that they were three races? Common history, language, literature, customs, even physical appearance gave that the lie. So Catholics are now visibly one race—Greek, Roman, English. We know it, feel it, love it. Who then dare blame us for care in keeping this our treasure and our life unsullied, undamaged, unlost till the day of full communion?

But how will that day come? Milner-White believed that it would come through the Anglican Communion becoming unified in a sacramental Catholicism which was intellectually free, and through Rome becoming willing to face the facts of history and the implications of freedom. Hence the importance meanwhile of the Anglican witness.

> The strength of our catholic witness lies just in the fact that our catholicism is *free*, and embraced voluntarily by free intellects; held not against new knowledge, new truth, but with it, because of it, inspired and mightily enriched by it. Catholicism is truth, and all truth is at home in Catholicism. But to make this plain and evident in an ever-changing world, *there must exist a Catholicism which is progressive.* The last hundred years have deluged the world with new knowledge ... I say outright that it is not more important to carry the Gospel through the worlds of heathendom than it is to carry the Gospel through these new worlds of

knowledge. That is the task for which English Catholicism alone
has the necessary freedom.

Meanwhile it is the Anglican task to show how intellectual freedom may
co-exist with the revival of supernatural religion.

> The battle for the Blessed Sacrament has been almost won; a deep
> devotional life centres round the weekly, nay the daily altar. The
> battle for the Sacrament of Penance has been half won. There are
> other central doctrines, however, such as a living consciousness
> of the Communion of Saints, where our work has hardly begun
> . . . . That is our contribution to unity with Rome—to establish
> here, in the United States and in the Dominions and perhaps
> more widely still, a true and deep Catholicism, deliberately
> chosen by thinking and educated people as the most loving and
> reasonable form of Christ's religion: a *tolerant* Catholicism ready
> and eager to marry again in the Church of S. Peter, when Rome is
> convinced by the Holy Spirit that the authority of love and reason
> is not only possible but true.

The far better known work of *One God and Father of All*, written in reply
to Father Vernon's polemic after his conversion to Rome, shows out more
fully the thesis of this address. But the widest aspects of Church and
Unity, as well as Church and Civilization, were treated in Milner-White's
contribution to *Essays Catholic and Critical*. Here he describes through
the centuries the Church's power of recovery and adaptation, its impact
upon culture and the tensions which that impact involves. Those who
read this essay probably remember less the main argument than some of
the epigrammatic sentences and the note of optimism which resounds
through it.

> The true history of the Church has never been written in human
> book, and never will be; for it has taken place not in courts, curias
> and councils where power is great and decisions are registered,
> but in cottages, streets and places where men work and pray.

The Renaissance and the Reformation are not truly two movements, two awakenings, this intellectual and that spiritual, but two sides of one. The godliest deed of those unpleasing fifteenth century popes was their welcoming of pagan thought ... Renaissance and Reformation act and counteract, influence and counter-influence, hurt and counter-hurt, mingle, achieve, transform, and yet leave huge tasks for the centuries of rest to work out after the centuries of tumult pass.

The work of the Church of England through the scientific and critical revolution has been at least of an importance sufficient to justify at the bar of history her position in temporary separation from the fellow Communion of East and West.

This sacrament to the world (the Church) will only be complete when it becomes the world, and the Royal Priesthood is universal.

In retrospect the chapter in *Essays Catholic and Critical* seems significant as presenting the Catholic Church less as an institution than as a life, less as a fenced terrain than as a light able to penetrate and pervade. Though Milner-White was never a close student of Eastern Orthodox writers his mind was in this respect akin to some of them. He inclined to a mystical rather than a legalistic approach towards Protestantism and the Free Churches. If he always believed firmly in apostolic succession and inherited something of the older self-consciousness of Church and Dissent, he was never legalistic in his attitude to unity. He saw the process as one of the sharing of spiritual treasures, and he would make easy rather than hard the acceptance by others of Catholic inheritance. He gave much thought to a form of *agape* as a desirable prelude to the day of intercommunion with the Free Churches. In later years he rejoiced in his work with Free Churchmen on the New English Bible, and one of his last acts in the Convocation of York was to support the scheme for Church Union in Ceylon. He was no less jealous for the liberty of the Church to govern her own life, though he never supported pleas for Disestablishment.

I have recalled Milner-White's writings of the 1920s as they show him as a creative exponent of the Liberal Catholicism of the time, and of those deep and lasting Anglican principles which lay beneath it. But theology was not to be his *métier*. Partly through the constant claim of pastoral concerns, partly through modesty and diffidence about himself *vis-à-vis* the theologians in Cambridge, partly through an absorbing interest in the arts of the Church, Milner-White appeared to take for granted the theological ground on which his life and work rested and to eschew the concern for the fundamental thinking for which he has himself pleaded eloquently. What was true of him was true of others too. I remember Edwyn Clement Hoskyns, who had embraced wholeheartedly the work of New Testament scholarship, lamenting that men as gifted as Geoffrey Clayton and Milner-White had "deserted" theology for pastoralia. Certainly Milner-White produced at King's many devoted priests but very few theologians, and he never took care to secure a tradition of theological teaching in the College.

Some of us who were theologically concerned were critical of a *lacuna* which we felt to exist in Milner-White's influence. In fact, as I discovered in conversations with him in his last years, Milner-White had often read much and thought deeply about some of the acute questions for faith; but having found peace of conviction he was anxious not to display knowledge of these conflicts or to worry his disciples with problems. It was, he believed, his mission to convey to others the joy and serenity of faith as he had come to possess it.

When the second great war of the century came, Milner-White had been at King's a long time. His influence had come to be felt widely in the Church, not least as a writer of prayers and as one who had led many to the priesthood. In Cambridge he began to seem tired and stale. The specific impulse of Liberal Catholicism had spent its force, and other movements were now more prominent. The Oratory of the Good Shepherd, abandoning its mother house to the Franciscans, was less of an intensive force in Cambridge and more a diffused influence in the wider Church. For all Milner-White's continuing achievement the glow of the earlier years had faded. He was inclined to be depressed and bewildered. Then there came, in 1941, the call to York.

The call to York was a gate to new vigour and achievement. It brought to the service of a great Cathedral, a Province, and the wider Church, those powers and principles which had been Milner-White's from the earlier years. I remember well the letter which he wrote to me (I had gone to Durham as Canon and Professor in the previous year) saying, "I follow you to the North, where there is life."

"The North, where there is life." Into the North Milner-White threw himself. The most vivid impression which I recall was he who *seemed* to be growing idle had become one of the most hard-working men alive. As a neighbour in Durham and latterly as a nearer neighbour in Bishopsthorpe, I was astonished at the sheer volume of work accomplished—the care of the Minster and its worship, the glass and the fabric, the young academic institutions in the City, northern schools, the army in the North, liturgical work, the translation of the Bible, hobbies old and new, and all the while the priest and the cure of souls. It was all possible because at the heart of it there was the discipline and the serenity of a Christian and a priest.

So the York years were the fruition in a larger life of the ideals of churchmanship and religion which had been Milner-White's from the beginning and had their first flowering in the early days of Cambridge and the first war. There were no doubt aspects of the Northern community which Milner-White hardly touched, and no doubt limitations in his touch. The old shyness was never lost. Yet in the York years there was an outgoing energy of influence and a witness to the bearing of Christianity on life and culture, with the worship of the Minster as the heart and centre. With the care for beauty in worship there went the care that the people who used the Minster should find expressed there *their* prayer and praise as they offered *their* concerns to the divine goodness.

Let this be the place to recall Milner-White's long concern for forms of worship, and for the language of prayers. He was not a scientific liturgiologist in the ordinary sense of the word. His supreme interest was in forms of service outside those of the Prayer Book, with their immense evangelistic opportunity, and in the language and diction of the prayers.

As to forms of service Milner-White's concern goes back to his chapters on the subject in *The Church in the Furnace*. In that war-time essay he pleaded, from his experience in the camps and the trenches, for services relevant, brief, more easily prayable, and giving room for the *affective* element in devotion. Something of what he was asking found expression in *Cambridge Offices and Orisions* (1921). This little book continues to be reprinted and used, no doubt, by reason of its skill in adapting to new needs and occasions the traditional form of the short "office", with a remarkable skill in the provision of scriptural versicles and responses. The same kinds of skill reappear in the new edition of the *Cuddesdon Office Book* on which Milner-White bestowed great pains. Those works prepared the way for the many "special services" devised for York Minster. These deserve to be collected and reprinted as a guide for the avoidance of pitfalls which beset such compositions. I would recall an article which Milner-White wrote for *The York Quarterly*, February 1959, with the title "Special Services: A Liturgical Need". Here we find discussed the needs of Structure, Form, and Language to be considered by those who design special services. "Not for one moment", he concludes, "can a Christian *learn* worship from those specialised devotional acts, but he can be introduced to the full liturgy of the Church by their interest, their faith and their immediate bearing upon actual living. And if their standards of structure, form and expression impress, already fresh gateways are opened into the invisible, the spiritual and the eternal which our material society so sorely needs." Milner-White believed strongly in the missionary impact of well-devised acts of worship.

As to the writing of prayers Milner-White's work covers a similarly long period as his concern with forms of service. He regarded the 1928 Prayer Book as a notable contribution to liturgical advance and regretted its defeat in Parliament; but he came to be very critical of the diction of many of the new prayers in it and his criticism spurred his own efforts. His ideas are largely set out in the essay on "Modern Prayers and their Writers" which he contributed to *Liturgy and Worship* (1932) as well as in the pamphlet *The Occasional Prayers of the 1928 Book Reconsidered*. In his own compositions he had regard to the varieties of form available— the collect and others. He was liable in his writing of prayers, as in his other activities, to slip on occasion into caricaturing himself, and at their worst his prayers could be too "precious". At their best they have proved incisive, useable, and lasting. Some of his own prayers, and more well-chosen prayers of others from many sources are collected in his *After the Third Collect*, widely used in Churches and widely influential. No less widely used has been the collection made with private prayer in view, *Daily Prayer*, in which he collaborated with Canon G. W. Briggs.

Milner-White was more than a compiler of prayers. He was concerned to lead others in the spirit of prayer, and in that way of contemplation which is nearer to daily life than many people realize. A few years before his death he published a book in which he shared with his readers something of the intimacy of his own approach to prayer, *My God my Glory*. It is a series of meditative pieces which, he explains, "have not been written, but have grown in many years, out of many meditations, many needs and one desire". The author provides his readers not with prayers so much as words which frame the desire for God in many moods and occasions. Only a man of prayer, of simplicity and sincerity, could wish to write such a book, and it will bring great help to those who will use it in the spirit in which it is written. It is a book which brings contemplation near to the circumstances of every day.

If these writings on prayer and worship are the key to Milner-White's wider influence, they are also not far from the secret of York Minster in his time. He found there a tradition already developed by Dean Ford and Dean Bate, which he was able to deepen and widen: a worship which was itself an evangel not by self-conscious efforts to be missionary but by unselfconscious service of God and of the people who were drawn in. Perhaps in Milner-White's time the three great features of the Minster worship were the Solemn Eucharist on Sundays and Holy Days, the many services for the people on special occasions, and the quiet orderliness of all that was done. But the outward and visible had beneath it the inner discipline which the Dean shared with those who worked with him.

In his early years Milner-White's churchmanship had been a mixture of tradition and adventure, and so it was to the end. But I cannot close upon any solemn note, for Milner-White had far more than most men the gift of laughing at himself. That gift was part of the serenity of faith into which he helped many to find their way.

EU GPSR Authorized Representative:

LOGOS EUROPE, 9 rue Nicolas Poussin, 17000 La Rochelle, France

contact@logoseurope.eu

www.ingramcontent.com/pod-product-compliance
Ingram Content Group UK Ltd.
Pitfield, Milton Keynes, MK11 3LW, UK
UKHW020917240425
457797UK00014B/62/J